Were You Always an Italian?

ANCESTORS AND OTHER
ICONS OF
ITALIAN AMERICA

Were You Always an Italian?

ANCESTORS AND OTHER
ICONS OF
ITALIAN AMERICA

Maria Laurino

W. W. NORTON & COMPANY

New York *London*

"Piazza Navona" reprinted by permission of Lousiana State University
Press from *Sonnets of Giuseppe Belli*, translated, with an Introduction, by Miller
Williams. Translation copyright © 1981 by Miller Williams.

"Mambo Italiano" written by Bob Merrill. Copyright © 1954, renewed
1982, Golden Bell Songs.

Excerpts from "In Paradise" poem from *The Hidden Italy*, by Hermann W.
Haller, reprinted by permission of Wayne State University Press ©.

For information about permission to reproduce selections from this book,
write to Permissions, W. W. Norton & Company, Inc., 500 Fifth Avenue,
New York, NY 10110

The text of this book is composed in Centaur MT.
Composition by Allentown Digital Services Division
of R.R. Donnelley & Sons Company
Manufacturing by The Haddon Craftsmen, Inc.
Book design by Judith Abbate

Library of Congress Cataloging-in-Publication Data
Laurino, Maria.
Were you always an Italian? : ancestors and other icons
of Italian America / Maria Laurino.
p.   cm.
Includes bibliographical references (p.   ).
ISBN 0-393-04930-2
1. Laurino, Maria. 2. Italian Americans—Biography.
3. Italian American women—Biography. I. Title.
E184.I8 L38 2000
973'.0451'0092—dc21
[B]   00-026028

W. W. Norton & Company, Inc., 500 Fifth Avenue, New York, N.Y. 10110
www.wwnorton.com

W. W. Norton & Company Ltd., 10 Coptic Street, London WC1A 1PU

4 5 6 7 8 9 0

FOR MY PARENTS AND MY BROTHERS
AND TONY AND MICHAEL, OF COURSE

Questo è il punto: rendere espliciti i rapporti
col mondo che ognuno di noi porta con sé, e che oggi
si tendono a nascondere, a far diventare inconsci, credendo
che in questo modo spariscano, mentre invece . . .

This is the point: to make explicit the relationship
with the world that each of us bears within himself,
and which today we tend to hide, to make unconscious,
believing that in this way it disappears, whereas . . .

—ITALO CALVINO, *Difficult Loves*

Contents

Were You Always an Italian?

ANCESTORS AND OTHER
ICONS OF
ITALIAN AMERICA

Beginnings

ONCE MANY, MANY YEARS AGO, in a small village named Conza della Campania in the province of Avellino, my maternal great-grandfather Michele Conte fell in love with the younger of two daughters, but by tradition he was obligated to marry the older sister, Concetta. He followed the rules of the southern Italian village, and Concetta bore him two children, my grandfather Natale and, some years later, his brother Antonio. Still, Michele couldn't resist the beauty of Concetta's younger sister, and he had a daughter by this woman.

As her sister's belly expanded, my great-grandmother grew more and more agitated, until she became very ill. My great-grandfather, in a loveless marriage and deeply unhappy at the prospect of living with a mentally unstable woman, placed his wife in a home for lunatics that was run by local nuns. Under the sisters' watch and care Concetta Conte remained there, I am told, for the rest of her days, sitting quietly in a chair weaving lace, each pull and tug of the thread a sedative for the pain. My great-grandfather journeyed on his own to America to find work on the railroad and raise enough money to send for his young sons, Natale and Antonio. But he was killed on the job and the two boys had to fend for themselves in Conza.

In this same village, my great-grandmother Rosa La Riccia was married to Michele Cantarella, a difficult, ill-tempered man. She bore him my grandmother Maria, my great-uncle Pasquale, and twins who died in childbirth. After the arduous labor of the still births, my great-grandfather sent Rosa back to work in the fields, but she was extremely weak and soon died of a hemorrhage. Michele got remarried, to a cruel woman who as a stepmother routinely beat her children.

Upon this vale of tears my maternal grandparents Natale Conte and Maria Cantarella met, teenagers deprived of their mothers. They married in 1906, when they were both twenty years old. A few years later, my grandfather left southern Italy for America to earn enough money to send for his wife, her brother Pasquale, and his brother. Antonio, barely a teenager, was fearful of making the trip, and decided to stay behind. The brothers corresponded but never met again. My grandfather insisted that he would one day return to southern Italy to retire, but he died years before his dream could take place. No one from my immediate family had ever seen the town of Conza della Campania until I traveled there in 1996 to visit Antonio's children.

These are the tales that have been told to me. The truth that remains is the truth of one hundred years of time.

AVELLINO IS 165 MILES SOUTH of Rome; Conza della Campania is a little over 40 miles east of Avellino, resting mid-ankle on the southern boot. My father's family lived further south in the province of Potenza, in the town of Picerno. Before I had traveled south, I felt a stronger tie to Avellino than to Potenza, strangely connected to it. I had heard my mother speak of "provinch d'Avelline," using a dialect pronunciation. Provinch d'Avelline, she said, drawing the words close together with a certainty that has made her the standard-bearer of her parents' memories. Without ever having seen the land, she confidently claimed the hazy space between possession and loss, the knowledge of a palpable yet irretrievable past.

I may have shared my mother's sense of belonging because I look more like her than like my father. I cannot forget a conversation with a man I met years ago in Rome's Piazza Navona, who, after talking to me for a few minutes, knowing only that I was Italian-American, said, "You look like all the girls from Avellino." In the Eternal City, I learned that my face had both a history and a future. The past becomes more real when a physical trail leads us to it.

The journey from Conza to Avellino once took a day and a half by donkey and two-wheeled cart. Transportation improved in 1895, when the first railway was built and one slow erratic train chugged between the small farming village and the provincial capital. My mother's parents probably went to Avellino only a few times in their lives, where they would have obtained the essential papers to leave for America.

Scents

ICAN STILL REMEMBER THE day when my ethnicity no longer felt like the tag line of my narrative, reluctantly affixed to my American self, but instead signified an inescapable me. I was a teenager standing in line before gym class, and we began to strut in sync, bare legs and barely covered bodies, to the gymnasium. Our uniforms were the baby blue of surgeons' gowns and prison uniforms. I felt both sick (or I feigned physical illness) and trapped (excuses about stomachaches rarely worked) during those fifty forced minutes of exercise.

Gym class, humiliating gym class, had provoked earlier difficult episodes. Once, in junior high—that particular place and time in which sameness is the prize, and a seed of adolescent difference could sprout into a field of skunk cabbage—a blond girl who had already developed curves that had captured the attention of a league of boys mentioned with a bored nonchalance how she needed to shave her legs. The blond girl's legs were as smooth and silky as a newly varnished oak floor, and I couldn't imagine why she'd put a razor to her skin. The hair on my legs, however, looked like a bed of wilted grass dipped in black ink.

"I need to shave too," I naïvely replied. To share the truth—that my mother thought I was too young to have a woman's legs—would have been mortifying, but I also lacked the instinct to distract her with a line like "You know, Cybill Shepherd couldn't hold a candle to your thighs," and quickly change the topic. The look of horror on that girl's face when she peered down at my calves is as clear to me today as it was back then in 1973. I'm sure she had never encountered the hirsute beauty of the Italian-American body.

The girl, too young to be tactful, revealed her thoughts in wide-eyed disbelief. At about the same time, I received a more discreet reaction to my appearance from a motherly neighbor who casually mentioned that I should bleach my dark arm hair blond. For much of my childhood I stood out in homogenized suburbia (hard as I tried to mask the Italian side of my hyphen); I grew up in a neighborhood where, in every other home, Mazola poured from clear plastic bottles, while we lifted heavy golden-colored tins of olive oil. To a child who wished to imitate others with the precision of a forger's brush, that was a clumsy, humiliating distinction. While such incidents embarrassed me, none was as difficult as this conversation before gym class:

"You were shopping at Saks the other day?" the popular girl next to me asked.

"Uh-huh," I meekly replied. (She had never spoken to me before; in retrospect the visit to Saks probably provided a necessary credential.)

"Yeah, I told my mother, 'That's the smelly Italian girl who stands in front of me in gym class.'"

I was stunned. I didn't move quickly enough in class even to perspire. But instead of challenging her, I just stood there.

Silently. As she continued to chatter, I yearned to shed my smell, my self, that very instant. Standing in the powerless world of childhood, a world in which the words and actions of peers cast the parts that we play for years, I intuitively understood that I was bound to the sweat of my ancestors, peasants from southern Italy. Even the name of the region, the Mezzogiorno, or "midday," invokes an oppressive afternoon heat that parches the skin and then showers it with drops of sweat.

Yet despite my deep self-consciousness, the part of me that recognized the significance of a school social hierarchy was flattered: this pretty, popular girl was talking to me. Sloe-eyed with chocolate brown hair, she was Jewish; I could never be like the Waspy girls, but I could see myself as a darker, rawer version of her. We were both slightly above average height, but she was thin, shaved her legs, plucked her eyebrows, and dyed unwanted lip hairs blond with a jar of Jolene. I, on the other hand, was chubby, and had the leg hairs of a grizzly, a light mustache, and a bristly black feather of an eyebrow that rested proudly at the bottom of my forehead.

Comparing our basic similarities, I saw the potential for my own reform. So I decided that if she continued to befriend me, I would ignore the nasty comment. In the following weeks, I tried to ingratiate myself into her world and she began to accept me. But always she'd tell classmates about the incident that sparked our first conversation. "I saw her shopping at Saks," she would say with a high-pitched giggle, "and I told my mother, 'That's the smelly Italian girl who stands in front of me in gym class.'"

She never talked about the smelly girl, or that smelly girl who is Italian, but rather that "smelly Italian girl"—in other words, I was smelly *because* I was Italian. She also acted surprised to have seen me at Saks; with a popular girl's unfailing instinct for the social ladder, perhaps she found it amusing that an Italian girl, who should have been on the bottom rung, would shop in the town's fanciest store.

Soon sympathetic friends pulled me aside to say that I never smelled and she must have confused me with someone else. I burned with embarrassment, but politely nodded as they defended me. Looking back on those days, I must have believed them, since I did not begin to shower three times a day to escape my odors. Instead, I continued the same bath regimen (although I can't say precisely if it was every day or every other) and sprayed myself with a fragrance called Love's Fresh Lemon, marketed for teens with a popular Donovan song about wearing your love like heaven. Did I smell like hell and rotten lemons? Probably not. Rather than believing that I smelled, I accepted the definition of being smelly. That is, if someone thought I had a body odor, there must be something unpleasant about me that needed to be changed.

Gym class wasn't the only time I heard the words "Italian" and "smelly" placed together, like a pungent clove of garlic sweating in a pan of warm olive oil. A few months later, I was sitting in the cafeteria with my new gym pal and a friend of hers, sharing gossip and news between bites of our sandwiches. The other girl mentioned that her father was planning a trip to Italy, and my friend and I swayed in delight at the idea of traveling to Europe.

"Are you going with him?" we asked in an enthusiastic chorus.

"Are you kidding?" she replied with a girlish laugh. "And be around all those smelly Italians?"

SUELLEN HOY, THE AUTHOR of a book on cleanliness, tells this anecdote: In 1957, when she was a teenager and had recently begun to shave, she was lounging at a pool with several other bare-legged friends. There they saw an older woman in a beautiful bathing suit reveal her hairy legs and armpits. Hoy was "shocked and repulsed" to see this woman's unsightly hair in public, and her girlfriends decided that the woman must be "foreign" because European women didn't shave. The incident, Hoy explains, first taught her about America's obsession with being clean. Not much has changed—she also cites a "Dear Abby" column from 1985 in which a reader advises that if " 'Rapunzel Legs' [is] too lazy to shave, she should move to Europe." Another woman wrote in that Europeans who don't shave also "think sweat and other natural body odors are sexy. Pee-ooey!"

It may be a peculiarly American habit to associate leg hair with dirt. Ultimately, however, looking dark and unkempt because of unwanted body hair is very different from being called smelly. I wonder if I earned that label because I seemed more foreign than the rest of the girls in my class. Not that we were recent Italian immigrants; I am third-generation, the youngest of my grandparents' youngest-born. Yet around the same time as the gym incident, a teacher who called out my name for attendance on the first day of class asked if I spoke English.

The label "smelly Italian" was acceptable to many teenagers in my high school for another reason: body odor suggests that you are ill-bred, a member of the lower class. For centuries, the sweet scents of the upper class and the earthy smells of the lower class differentiated both groups in body and spirit. More than the clothes one wears or the language one speaks, the stink that fills the air of an unwashed person, the dirt and sweat that turn underarms and loins into a triangular estuary of odor, a repository of the unwanted emissions of our bodies, separates the classes. The "basement odor of the masses," as Flaubert once wrote, serves as one of the clearest demarcations between rich and poor.

The issue of smell and class plagued George Orwell for many years. In *The Road to Wigan Pier*, his treatise for a socialist state, Orwell wrote with characteristic bluntness that there are "four frightful words which people nowadays are chary of uttering," that is, "the lower classes smell." Orwell reasoned that class equality could never be achieved if the bourgeoisie continued to consider the lower classes "inherently dirty," making olfactory distinctions between *us* and *them*. Such a judgment can be impenetrable, he claimed, because a physical feeling of dislike is far more difficult to transcend than an intellectual one.

Orwell may have paid particular attention to odors because as a child he had his own fears that he smelled bad. Describing his experiences as a scholarship student in an elite public school, Orwell wrote in his essay "Such, Such Were the Joys . . .": "A child's belief in its own shortcomings is not much influenced by facts. I believed, for example, that I 'smelt,' but this was based simply on general probability. It was notorious that disagreeable people smelt, and therefore presumably I did so too."

Orwell thought that he was "disagreeable" because his family was poorer than those of the other boys at his school, who came from the highest quarters of English society. The writer, with his flawless understanding of England's class system, famously described his family's economic status as "lower-upper-middle class." But because class distinction is relative and children want more than anything to be like their peers, Orwell must have imagined that a lower-class boy smelled—and that he took on this trait.

I may have accepted my classmates' assumptions because my family's economic position could be described as deep in the basement of upper-middle-class life, or, more accurately, we lived a middle-middle-class life—in the strict American sense of annual income. (Orwell came from an established English family whose fortunes had dwindled.) The notion that I was called smelly because I was Italian seemed as logical a matter of cause and effect as that I was chubby because I ate brownies at lunch. Growing up in Short Hills, New Jersey, a suburb that produced debutantes just as Detroit manufactured steel, I learned as a child that the shrill whistle sounding every hour at the station signaled more than an approaching train: the town's dividing line was drawn at the railroad, and we were on the wrong side of the tracks. While many of my friends lived in sprawling ranch houses with stone patios and outdoor pools, our little split-level house in a new development had a modest lawn that blended into the same-sized property of our neighbors, who were mostly small businessmen, middle managers, and teachers. As my neighborhood pal would remind me, we lived in "the ghetto of Short Hills."

Perhaps any child who is poor among the rich learns to kowtow to the needs of the wealthy, and in doing so carries a deep sense of shame over her own inadequacies. The child intuits the sense of privilege that the rich share, and knows she'll be rewarded by indulging them, commenting on how lovely their house is, oohing and aahing at the wall of mirrors in the bathroom, enthusiastically accepting the gracious invitation to swim in their pool. Her role is to be a constant reminder, like a grandfather clock that chimes reassuringly, of just how much they have.

But people pride themselves on degrees of wealth, so I never forgot that the real "ghetto" was in a section of Millburn, the neighboring town where my father had grown up, that housed an enclave of Italian-Americans. Because Short Hills was part of Millburn Township, the poor kids and young gents went to school together (the public school was so good that there was not the usual channeling of the elite to private schools). In both junior high and high school, there were mainly middle-, upper-middle-, and upper-class teens. Latinos and African-Americans were still excluded back then, so the only people of color in my high school were the children of the housekeeper at the local Catholic church. That left the largest dark ethnic group: the lower-middle-class Italians from Millburn, and the only kids labeled with an ethnic slur.

In high school, the Italian-American boys were known as the "Ginzo Gang"; they were greasers with beat-up cars that first chugged, then soared, thanks to their work at the local gas station (Palumbo's), owned by the father of one of them. Olive-skinned and muscular, they were sexy in their crudeness; and their faint gasoline scent and oiled-down hair defined the image of Italian-Americans in our school. The young women who hung out with them had little separate identity other than as the girlfriends of the Ginzos.

The Ginzos were my rearview mirror, a reflection of the near past that I wished to move beyond. They were an acknowledgment of my heritage, a recognition that the small sum of money my mother had inherited from her parents, used as the down payment on our house in a neighborhood a mile away, allowed me to escape from their world. But who was I fooling? My grandfather, who started a small construction company, earned his money by digging the earth; sweat and dirt were part of me, an oath of fealty to my family's peasant past. Yet I preferred to bury the memories of his labor, which provided us with some material comforts but not enough to rid me of the label of the "smelly Italian girl."

In the interval between the accusation of being smelly and an unspoken admission of my guilt, a denial of my ethnic self emerged. Unprepared to confront my fears, I responded like a criminal who'd do anything to get the charges dropped. If the cause of being called smelly were my Italian roots, then I would pretend not to be Italian.

At first I rejected the smells of my southern European heritage. Gone were the tastes and aromas of my youth: the sweet scent of tomato sauce simmering on the stove, soothing as a cup of tea on a rainy night; the paper-thin slices of prosciutto, salty and smooth on the tongue; and my own madeleine, oil-laden frying peppers, light green in color with long, curvaceous bodies that effortlessly glide down the throat and conjure up memories of summer day trips to Asbury Park, where we ate ham, Swiss, and fried pepper sandwiches prepared by my mother. Instead, I began to savor the old flavors of eastern Europe, new to my tongue: pickled herring and cured fish, sour and smoky, and the brisket I was served when I ate holiday meals with my new friend from gym class.

Decades later, when I told my Jewish husband that in high school I tried to assimilate by imitating his culture, he laughed. But in the uninformed world of the adolescent, narrow assumptions get made about the scheme of things. At the time, I didn't understand that the Jewish girls who zealously booked plastic surgery appointments with Howard Diamond, the Manhattan doctor famous for creating identical pug noses in Short Hills and Great Neck, Long Island, were undergoing a similar identity struggle.

Stripped of familiar smells, next I wanted to eliminate the extra baggage of vowels, those instant markers of ethnicity.

"Mom, why did you name me Maria?" went my familiar dinner-table question.

"Hun, why did we choose Maria?" she'd say, deferring to my father. He had wanted to name me Denise, after a Belgian child who greeted his troop during World War II and remained etched in his memory.

"Mama's name was Maria," my mom would add, interrupting her own question and recognizing that she was the keeper of tradition, the holder of the deciding vote. "Your father's mother was Maria, and I loved the actress Maria Montez."

Her last explanation was the consolation prize, the frayed ticket to the American scene that she had won and wished to hand to me. Naming me after a beautiful, vapid actress (Spanish, no less) would have revealed an unseen side of my mother, one that had rebelled against the expectation of having to show respect. A momentary fantasy, a chimera. I'm certain that I was named after my mother's mother.

But I would adopt the Montez interpretation. That both my grandmothers were named Maria bore little relevance at the time; a grade B movie actress, however, at least sounded glamorous.

"Why didn't you change our last name to Laurin?" I continued in my teenage whine. During these end-of-the-day efforts to sanitize myself, washing off an *o* seemed a clean, decisive stroke.

Only years later did I begin the precarious work of trying to replace the layers of ethnicity I had stripped away in order to dissociate myself from the smelly Italians. The alien surroundings of college fostered a nostalgia for familiar tastes and allowed me to appreciate the foods I had grown up with, although not everyone shared my enthusiasm. Once my freshman roommate approached me, her face a picture of compassion and concern, as I entered our tiny dorm room. How was my weak stomach? she asked. Momentarily befuddled, I soon realized that she had confused the pungent aroma of the provolone I had recently eaten with that of vomit, and believed that I had thrown up in our room.

By my early twenties, I learned more about the girl at the cafeteria table who talked about the smelly Italians. According to the local grapevine, her parents were getting divorced because her father had been making seasonal trips to Italy to visit his secret mistress and their two children. Now I realize that she probably was never invited on her father's frequent sojourns, and the thought-less remark was the defense of an insecure child, rejected by a man too busy sniffing the earthy scents of Italians to spend much time with her.

TODAY I HAVE A new fear about smell; I fear that I lack a defining odor. I feel removed from my own sense of smell and the images it could conjure. I feel a languorous appreciation for every-day scents, like my pots of dried lavender, whose wildflower fra-grance has faded to a docile sachet, as its deep purple buds grew pale with streaks of beige, a graceful bow to domesticity and old age. I refuse to linger by the coffeepot and sniff my carefully chosen beans, or inhale their smoky end, first ground, then mud-died and scorched by a hot rain; instead, I quickly dump the grounds and wash the pot in soapy water, just as I will rush to lather the summer heat off my body. No smell, no mess. Life is measured, careful, far removed from the chaos of dirt and its primitive pleasures, and the smelly label of my youth.

Clean, but without texture; scrubbed of the salty drops that tell our singular stories. I fear that after years of trying to rid my-self of the perceived stench of my ethnic group and its musty-basement-class status, I sanitized my own voice, washed it away.

Certain incidents in life—like being told during gym class that you smell—become emotional markers, and around these events a series of reactions are set in motion: giving up pizza for pickled herring can take years to undo. I have recently come to notice how much time I spend scenting my body, covering it with colognes, milks, and creams, giving it a pleasant but artificial character, or voice, you could say. At first I was unaware that I had become perfume-obsessed, as people can often be unaware of their obsessions. But now I think I can link its beginnings to a time and a place.

Initially, I didn't realize the connection between a fragrance fixation and a freelance writing career, but neither did I fully understand that a spray of cologne can provide a narrative for your body in case your own story lacks luster. My aromatic addiction began when I decided not to return (after a brief stint in government) to the newspaper I had worked at for nearly a decade, which was as familiar as family. I was nervous about the decision to freelance, because it not only took away an important piece of identity but would force me to choose my subjects, instead of writing about what others expected of me. And perhaps even worse, telling people that you are a full-time freelancer sounds more like a euphemism for unemployment than an adult career choice. So I acted a bit like the child who leaves home for the first time: one part wants to go while the other kicks and drags his way down the stairs, clutching the newel post. The final decision to step out the door and not return to my old work home coincided with a surprise birthday gift from my husband, a five-day trip to Paris. A perfect distraction, except that I found myself spending a good part of the time thinking about a particular French cologne.

I would like to chalk it up to coincidence rather than to Freud that I had occasionally been wearing a French cologne with a light lemon scent and Roman emperor's name, Eau d'Hadrien, which seemed like an elegant version of the Love's Fresh Lemon of my youth. But maybe the alchemy of a new affection for Europe and my old need to hide Italian smells with lemons conjured an odd sensory experience—reluctance, relief!—when I first sniffed this cologne.

I went to a small Left Bank perfumery filled with fluted glass bottles capped in gold and bought my scent, one of my tasks in Paris, because it was cheaper there than back home. The saleswoman handed me the bag and then made an irresistible gesture:

she sprayed my body, from my neck to my thighs, with cologne. Her hands flowed gently yet confidently around me, and the idea of being covered in fragrance, not frugally dabbed behind the ears, was so enticing that I went back to the store every day for a purchase and another spray. I had discovered a scented balm to soothe a shaky ego.

"Is this a gift for someone?" she asked upon my return.

"No, it's for me," I happily responded, waiting for the soft mist to drape me like a gossamer veil.

After that trip, I became even more attached to the fragrance, or perhaps the idea of this fragrance. In department stores, I allowed myself one indulgent purchase: hand cream, body lotion, perfumed body cream (my favorite—it's as if I'm covered in lemons and cream), soaps, other colognes to mix with my fragrance to create a new, layered smell—the possibilities seemed endless. I no longer just sprayed behind the ears but covered myself completely in the scent, letting the perfume conquer the blandness of a scrubbed self, an elixir to enliven a diffident voice.

I used to think that my guilt-free desire for an expensive French cologne meant that I was at least coming to terms with the embarrassing bourgeois side of myself, which capitalized on the chic of a European heritage rather than my real-life peasant roots. But now I realize that, like the young girl who wanted to deny her heritage, again I was ducking for cover. I never quite unlearned the lesson from gym class long ago, when the voices of my family and my past were silenced as I altered the scents surrounding me. It's easier to shower away a smell, to censor yourself with a scent, than to accept your body's signature, the rawness of odor and sweat.

The smelly Italian girl no longer exists, if she ever did. In addition to my fragrance, my body is practically hairless, waxed from lip to toe by a Gallic woman who says "Voilà" after finishing each leg and who reminisces about her country, sharing with me that she knows the colorist who knows the colorist who mixes the blond hair dye for Catherine Deneuve (her six strands of separation from true glamour). During the months between waxings, I let my leg hair grow long and I run my fingers through it, still mystified by the abundance of those dark strands that I wish to find beautiful, but that I ultimately decide to remove once again.

I have tried to escape the class boundaries of my youth, but sometimes, in that lonely space between me and the bathwater, I wonder what has become of my own smell, and what it would be like to uncover a voice that could tell the stories of my past.

Tainted Soil

THE ELUSIVE SEARCH FOR the past, the journey to understand the self not just in relation to a particular moment in time but to the many moments that preceded our consciousness, seems an impossible task when history is vague and conflicted, and shifts between two different lands. How do you recapture the past when knowledge is limited and molded by others? I cannot say that my life has been shaped only by my nuclear family and American education, or that the hundreds of years prior to my birth, years my relatives spent on southern Italian soil, have shed no influence on the person I now am. Don't we all, to borrow Virginia Woolf's words, "encounter instincts already acquired by thousands of ancestresses in the past"? But I have few guideposts to understanding life in southern Italy.

I have come to hate the books and documentaries about the "Italian-American experience," full of treacly discussions of food and family, describing "the beautiful song" of our heritage, those snapshots of golden days forever gone. Celebrities and politicians are the usual interview subjects; the former reminisce, and the latter repeat maxims and banalities like "We learned about self-sacrifice and respect for the family," and "We have a unique heritage." Are others taught selfishness? Don't all ethnic groups possess singular histories? These pasta/pizza/*paesano* tales embroider the myth of the "*italiano*," reshaping disparate character traits into a singular folkloric image, rendering us indistinguishable from each other, playing the Muzak of ethnicity.

Although I lament the dangers of selective nostalgia, I, too, willfully indulge in my family's tales of yesteryear. My mother, who has assumed the role of family storyteller, will describe a scene again and again, the repetition affirming the truth of the snapshot she presents: for instance, my maternal grandfather trying to teach his wife English, which he learned by reading the newspaper. "Veg-ah-TABLE, Maria, Veg-ah-TABLE," he said, emphatically slapping his hand on the kitchen table as he mispronounced the last syllable. My mother's mockery of the hopelessness of her father's English is tender, accompanied by admiration for a man who, I am told, defied the Depression through hard work, and whose warmth and good humor infused their apartment, along with the laughter of friends, the rhythms of swing music, and the comforting strum of his son's guitar. How different from the austere place I knew and hated to visit, my grandmother's mausoleum to him and their son; both were dead before I was three. In my memory of her dark apartment, I am alone in the pantry fingering a small tin baking sheet, the closest thing to a toy.

I will imagine my grandfather Natale and Uncle Mickey (Miguel, as my grandmother called him) as the gentlemen my mother has described; I feel obliged to preserve a memory that excludes me, to see the reels of the past through her voice, clear and strong, fluctuating with each detail and crescendoing to an excited high pitch by the end of the narrative. The portrait is contained, ensuring no conflict. When I choose to partake in this past, I am accepting a particular version of events—that her life was good (on wistful days she means better) before she was married, and that her father and brother, who both died too young, provided a warmth and humor that have never been replaced. These stories are usually told in the kitchen, fulfilling an Italian-American cliché, because that is the gathering place where we all sit closest together, five of us in assorted colored leather swivel chairs chosen when I was ten and, despite several deep tears in the red, gold, and avocado fabrics, never replaced.

At times when I am with my family and hear these stories, a hundred years can slip away, generations overlap like the tight fold of pleats: a word of dialect captures an emotion in its purest form; life is told with bread and wine; nothing has changed. Yet I cannot imagine a life more different from the one I live now than that of my ancestors.

Consumed by this desire to connect to a lost time and place, I've been quick to romanticize my family's history, eagerly gathering scattered tidbits, patching together facts and weaving stories to form the ornate quilt of imagination. In the early eighties, I met a Roman journalist, Daniela Palladini, who would become a good friend, on a trip she made to New York with an Italian psychologist. During our lunch together, the psychologist seemed to offer a piece of my past. Speaking simply with a very thick accent, he remarked, "The name Laurino—you must be from the Naples area."

"Yes, yes," I enthusiastically replied. "How did you know?"

"Oh, because there was a very famous man named Lauro from Naples. He owned all these sheeps."

"Sheep, how interesting," I said. He and Daniela, who spoke less English than the psychologist, smiled and nodded.

Sheep, I repeated to myself. I knew I had an agrarian past, but his declaration gave it a biblical aura. My grandfather the shepherd, descended from shepherds. I imagined small men wrapped in broad white sheets roaming dry land, their moist hands cupped over brow to shield their eyes from the blinding rays of the Mediterranean sun. I shared this nomadic yarn with my parents, who showed some interest, and anybody else who cared to listen. Years later, at a party that included several Italians, I began a conversation with a man who spoke much better English than the psychologist. Cornering him by a fireplace, I proudly repeated the story of my grandfathers the graziers: "I think I am somehow related to a man named Lauro who owned many sheep."

"Ships," he said, smiling wryly as he swirled his glass of white wine before taking the next sip.

"What?"

"Lauro was a shipping magnate."

My pastoral image plundered, I meekly continued the conversation until I could slink to the opposite end of the room, unable to hide a flushed pink face. Not only did I misunderstand the original story, but I should have recognized the name: the *Achille Lauro* had become famous because of the ruthless terrorist killing of an American aboard the cruise ship. The psychologist was suggesting that peasants from the Naples area were given the surname of the wealthy Lauro; I'm not sure if my father's family would have been one of these Laurinos, "little Lauros," since they lived hours away, in the region of Basilicata. And the psychologist's vowel confusion should have been apparent after he mentioned that he was at the "Hotel Peek-week," the Pickwick Hotel.

Without a fuller understanding of history, nostalgia fills the void and we become appendages to someone else's past, daylight somnambulists seeking peace with the spirits; or we create dangerous fictions, clutching a lost time that at all costs must be preserved undisturbed. In an impoverished American landscape of consumerism and technological hype, nostalgia has become a form of faith in a secular age, a palliative to replace the glare of the future with hazy yesterdays. In private we use nostalgia to find connections to help make sense of our lives; in public life nostalgia, if cleverly employed, offers a collective feel-good version of the past.

When I worked as a political reporter and later as a speechwriter, I watched (then helped) politicians rediscover the importance of personal nostalgia in a confessional age, using words like mosaic and tapestry to describe a universal ethnic experience, carefully choosing symbols to create a shared sense of belonging, applying a dose of cant to numb the burden of reality. In the last few decades, as Italian-American politicians have risen to prominence, they have reimagined the Italian experience and retold the immigrant struggle through the public forum. Their stories lack the subtle intricacies of psychological portraits or the ability to dissect honestly one's complex emotional relationship with the past; rather, the message is simple and inspiring: hard work and endurance make for strong character.

Some of these descendants of the south, given today's love affair with Italy, have reclaimed their heritage, as I once did, by leasing memories of a northern culture that meant little to their ancestors' lives. In a book called *Growing Up Italian*, Geraldine Ferraro, whose family was from southern Italy, talked about her son's studies in Florence, and concluded that when her children go to Italy "they enjoy the art, the architecture, the literature. They see the true component of their roots and are proud of them here." The true component of their roots? As Ann Cornelisen described the land south of Rome in *Women of the Shadows:* "The South's is *not* the gentle, terraced landscape of Renaissance painting. It is a bare, sepia world, a cruel world of jagged, parched hills, dry river beds and distant villages where clumps of low houses cling together on the edges of cutbanks." The majority of southern Italians share as much history with Florentines as girls from Appalachia would exchange with their Boston Brahmin "sisters."

Sometimes the political leader's choice of nostalgic symbols is weird and tinged with self-hate, such as New York Mayor Rudolph Giuliani's decision to dress in drag as an old Italian lady on national television and to show a screening of *The Godfather* for friends on New Year's Eve in celebration of his second mayoral inauguration. The steely former prosecutor announced to the press that the movie was his all-time favorite; perhaps he was seduced by Don Corleone's patriarchal rule rather than by the murders he plotted in the family name. The mayor/film critic's choice to ring in 1998 with the 1972 movie contrasted sharply with the decision former Governor Mario Cuomo made to distance himself from *The Godfather*'s portrayal of Italian-Americans. Cuomo understood the broad symbolism attached to serving in public office, and the first Italian-American governor of New York was not about to undermine the positive image of his ethnic group which he helped to create by condoning the stereotypic portrait of the mob thug.

Cuomo once told me in an interview: "John Lindsay never understood it, he never understood it. He invited me to the [mayor's] mansion to see *The Godfather* with Matilda. He was trying to get me to join his administration. I said, 'How can you invite me to see *The Godfather*? . . . This is the guy who kills people, murders them, plucks their eyes out, drugs them, and he's treated as a great guy, the whole community loves him. What are you saying with this movie?' " He recalled that Lindsay replied, "Oh, it's only a movie, you're too sensitive."

Mario Cuomo, who understood the importance of his role

as the most prominent intellectual southern Italian in American public life, probably was the most gifted practitioner of ethnic nostalgia. Using soothing yet shrewdly chosen words and imagery, Cuomo countered negative images that have plagued the Italian-American past.

I'll never forget a television performance by the former governor, who first gave me hope that Italian-American politicians were more than cheek-pinching, deal-making, behind-the-scenes players. The governor mesmerized my father during a Sunday morning interview show when he repeated a conversation he had had with his mother Immaculata. Cuomo was about to deliver his keynote address before the 1984 Democratic Convention, a speech that would bring him national recognition and lead to an eventual flirtation with the presidency.

"Ma, there may be forty to fifty million people who'll be watching," Cuomo said to his mother. As he retold the story, the old Italian woman responded cautiously, "Oh *marone*, you better not make a mistake."

Marone. The southern Italian derivation of Madonna, a call to the Virgin Mary that was clearly a mark of the lower class. It was one of the many Italian words I was taught never to say outside the home, yet a governor known for his eloquence had just announced it on television. As the governor said *marone*, I watched my father's eyes light up, his serious mouth forming an uncharacteristically wide grin. Perhaps he was imagining his own mother, Mariantonia, giving him practical and limited advice as Immaculata gave hers to Mario. My reaction was sentimental, mixed with an inchoate pride. As the peasant word shifted out of my private lexicon, it gained a legitimacy. And wanting to share my father's memories, I conjured up a grandmother I had never met.

The ethnic pride that Mario Cuomo presented to the public was personal, family-oriented, something he had discovered on his own. In his diaries, Cuomo surrounded himself with his culture, delighting the senses with descriptions of the salty, aromatic food that Italians savor: the four-foot provolone hanging in his father's store, the Genoa salami, prosciutto, and crusty bread. A trace of indignation colored his storyteller's voice as Cuomo told of the stigmatic wounds of his father, who "worked with his hands, bled from the bottom of his feet."

Cuomo chose the form of personal nostalgia because he never identified with a broader vision of the Italian-American past. The progressive legacy of the few Italian-American political heroes, like East Harlem's popular leaders Vito Marcantonio and his mentor, Fiorello La Guardia, the first Italian mayor of New York City, had faded when Cuomo came of age. Marcantonio was labeled a Communist, and La Guardia, who built the first public housing in the country and instituted a free milk program, was remembered as the boisterous ethnic reading the funny papers over the radio to children or brewing illegal beer to demonstrate the absurdity of Prohibition. Without positive images of the culture, Cuomo grew up reacting to ethnic slurs and ultimately identified with more cerebral heroes like Sir Thomas More and Abraham Lincoln.

"Were you always an Italian?" Mario Cuomo asked me some years ago.

His sententious question captured my own ethnic ambivalence. Cuomo was sitting in the ceremonial governor's office, a large, rarely used room in Albany restored to its ornate nineteenth-century splendor. His feet rested on a mahogany desk polished to a shiny luster, and he was leaning a little too far back to look entirely comfortable. To him, "being" Italian meant understanding the Mezzogiorno culture; being Italian meant overcoming the urge to hide the impoverished land of your ancestry. With childlike guilt, I shook my head no.

"I know all about ethnic-self hate," the Governor responded as he stood up to enter his real working office. Cuomo's background was similar to that of most children of immigrants who are unable to share the common experiences of their peers. As a teenager he was an outsider in a Catholic prep school: "They were all Irish. There were no Italian-Americans. There was nobody who shared my culture," he said. After he finished law school, tying for first place in his class, the dean suggested he change his name to get a Wall Street job. Years after the hurt of this comment had faded, Mario Cuomo the politician understood the story's universal appeal and loved retelling it to national audiences. "Can you imagine me as Mark Conrad?" began the governor's ethnic riff. "Just take a look at me, can you imagine me walking in and saying, 'Hi, I'm Mark Conrad'?" As Cuomo recalled the story for me, his tone was awkward, mechanical, showing the absurdity of adopting an Anglo-American model. "I play tennis. I play golf," he continued, extending a wood-tight arm in a make-belief handshake. No one would believe it, he laughed. And once in government office, Cuomo found himself defending the social fabric of his close-knit family.

As governor, Cuomo made us feel good, teaching us the immigrant lesson that hard work pays off. My parents smiled when Cuomo re-created the experience of his parents. He told us that the American dream could come true (it happened to him), borrowing from his Mezzogiorno history to create a delightful pastiche. The former governor chose his ethnic motifs just as a postmodern architect uses classical design to decorate a modern building; it was a playful twist, an accent, like the Philip Johnson Chippendale cleft and oversized Florentine arches that adorn the former AT&T Building. Words like *marone* chiseled his speech, Ionic columns on a postwar high-rise.

In a series of speeches that celebrated "the family of New

York," Cuomo described Tramonti, the southern Italian village of his mother, where the peasants lived in shacks with no heat and dirt floors and discovered a "strength, consolation, and survival in the sharing of benefits and burdens." Cuomo may not have had historical access to the workings of his mother's village, but the nostalgic image he rendered used the warm maternal image of Immaculata to counter the prevailing perception of Italians as self-serving and interested only in taking care of their own, a belief that had gained academic legitimacy with the publication of Harvard sociologist Edward Banfield's 1958 book, *The Moral Basis of a Backward Society.*

Banfield's fieldwork, which has been cited in academic circles for decades, led him to conclude that southern Italian peasants shared a common social trait, "amoral familism," or the inability to serve anyone outside the immediate family. After spending nine months in the southern Italian village of Chiaromonte, which he fictitiously named Montegrano (the town, deep in the hilly terrain of Lucania, now known as Basilicata, is in the same region where my paternal grandparents lived), the sociologist felt confident enough in the gestation of his theory to claim that "no one will further the interest of the group or community except as it is to his private advantage to do so." Banfield, who didn't speak the dialect and was aided by his wife Laura Fasano Banfield in interpreting the villagers' stories, added, "It is not too much to say that most people of Montegrano have no morality except, perhaps, that which requires service to the family."

"That the Montegranesi are prisoners of their family-centered ethos—that because of it they cannot act concertedly or in the common good," he concluded, "is a fundamental impediment to their economic and other progress." By divesting the political system that governed the peasants of its responsibility, Banfield's argument might be reduced in the nineties to: "It's their character, stupid." The blame-the-victim thesis, which the professor contrasted with the Anglo-American spirit of citizenship, led to some absurd conclusions: "The peasant's poverty is appalling to be sure, but it does not prevent him from contributing a few days of labor now and then to some community undertaking like repairing the orphanage."

Professors Nathan Glazer and Daniel Patrick Moynihan brought Banfield's thesis to the New World in their 1963 book, *Beyond the Melting Pot*, which argued that Italian-Americans are also amoral familists. In the section on Italian-Americans written by Nathan Glazer, the Harvard sociologist explained, "The content of this moral code remained basically the same among Italian immigrants to America. One should not trust strangers, and may advance one's interest at the cost of strangers. Also, one does not interfere with strangers' business. . . . [T]he contemporary American ethic values *self*-advancement, whereas the Italian variant still values *family* advancement. Thus, even in the case of Italian gangsters or racketeers, there is a surprising degree of family stability and concern with children, brothers, sisters, and other relatives." The seductive image of Glazer's concluding sentence, and his belief that the family-centered Italian-Americans were superior in running organized crime, prefigures the famous image of *The Godfather's* Don Corleone in which he conducts the family business during the elaborate spectacle of his only daughter's wedding.

By now, the concept of amoral familism has become so ingrained in the public consciousness that some people don't recognize its blatant racism. For generations, Italian-Americans have had to combat negative images about "family," which at worst is a euphemism for the Mafia, but amoral familism may be the more dangerous stereotype because it touches every member of the ethnic group. The idea of an inherent southern Italian selfishness, suggesting that the ethos of public service and the responsibilities of citizenship were beyond the immigrants' imagination, has buried memories of progressivism in America and followed Italian-Americans into the social isolation of the suburbs. William Sexton, a columnist for the Long Island newspaper *Newsday*, wrote that the gubernatorial years of Cuomo were plagued by "ethnic problems" like a "distrust of outsiders," and used the theories in *Beyond the Melting Pot* to bolster his argument.

"The qualities that endear Mario Cuomo to so many of us—the loyalty to family, the determination to be in command, the distrust of outsiders, the overriding self-confidence—they are the very factors weakening his administration," Sexton wrote. "These are ethnic qualities, and there are sociologists (among them most notably our own Pat Moynihan) who will tell you that they are the hallmarks of Italian family life, indeed the reason why Italian-American neighborhoods are so happily cohesive when the communal life of others seems to be falling apart. . . . In short—by this theory—it is no accident that Mario Cuomo was only the first Italian-American to win New York's governorship, more than a half a century after Irish-Americans sent Al Smith to Albany."

Is this management style a peculiarly Italian-American character trait—and a character trait that explains why Italian-Americans didn't hold high elective office for fifty years? Even successful Italian-American politicians were discounted by Glazer and Moynihan. They didn't consider La Guardia a truly Italian politician because he was raised as a Protestant and his mother was an Italian Jew (thirty-five years earlier, Walter Lippmann thought La Guardia quite Italian, commenting that his "sorry showing" of a mayoral campaign revealed "the real gap which lies between the Italian and the Anglo-American political tradition").

Glazer makes a passing reference to the East Harlemites, which included La Guardia, Marcantonio, educator Leonard Covello, and community activist Edward Corsi, as a *"sort of* Italian-American intelligentsia" (italics mine).

Cuomo rebutted the stereotype that Italians make good neighbors but not good governors; he embraced an image of the communal Italian family actively participating as citizens. When Cuomo was at his best, he gave the past immediacy and made people proud of their heritage while insisting that ethnic self-pride must coexist with respect for other races to produce "a wonderful mosaic." But voters grew tired of Cuomo's rhetoric and personal vision. He became known as the brilliant orator who couldn't channel his eloquent speech through the haze of Albany's petty politics; he was the clever postmodernist who could embellish the present with stories from the past, but who left office stymied by a Republican legislature and deprived of a substantive legacy, except perhaps his principled fight against the death penalty. And eventually his ethnicity became suspect. As governor, he was forced to answer vicious rumors that his father-in-law had mob connections, and the savvy politician sounded like a naïf when he once responded that the Mafia didn't exist.

Cuomo's own ambivalence denied him a place as a presidential candidate, and two years later he was defeated as governor. Political pundits whispered loudly that Cuomo may not have entered the New Hampshire primary because he feared that an endless stream of tabloid fictions built around Italian-American stereotypes would drag down a national candidacy. His nostalgic past had provided only temporary political capital, and ultimately withered next to the stubborn perception of amoral familism.

SINCE I FIRST READ Edward Banfield's *The Moral Basis of a Backward Society* over a decade ago, I have been haunted by his thesis and brutal word choice, this notion of a peasant "amorality" compared to the more virtuous traits of an Anglo-Saxon citizenry. Banfield's beliefs about southern Italy have been accepted as truth; only when he began writing about American cities did his racism become evident. In his 1970 book *The Unheavenly City* (a work that was so controversial he wrote a revised edition four years later), Banfield used the same "amoral familism" logic, positing that personal character traits, not poverty, define people and applying his theories to blacks in urban centers. His belief in an endemic lower-class character trait, what he termed their "present-orientedness," led him to a series of proposals for solving the problems of inner cities that included abolishing the minimum wage and lowering the graduation age to the ninth grade. "New schools may be built, new curricula devised, and the teacher-pupil ratio cut in half," writes Banfield, "but if the children who attend these schools come from lower-class homes, they will be turned into blackboard jungles, and those who graduate or drop out from them will, in most cases, be functionally illiterate."

The assumptions that Banfield, who served as chairman of Richard Nixon's task force on urban affairs and model cities, made in his books show the common thread that has long linked African-Americans and southern Italians, both victims of bias against racial and ethnic minorities, yet two groups that have never united as allies. In an isolated incident in 1974, Canadian black and Italian students came together in a protest organized by Students for a Democratic Society and physically blocked Banfield from speaking at the University of Toronto.

The controversy over *The Unheavenly City* did not diminish the acceptance among scholars of the concept of "amoral familism." Banfield's dated observations about the fatalistic culture of southern Italy were adopted in the 1990s by historian Francis

Fukuyama and political scientists James Q. Wilson and Robert Putnam. In *Making Democracy Work: Civic Traditions in Modern Italy*, Putnam, a Harvard professor and former dean of the Kennedy School, celebrates the "civic" culture of northern Italy by comparing its citizens to the "amoral individualists of the less civic" south. "Less civic" and "uncivic"—which sounds perilously close to "uncivilized"—are Putnam's unfortunate umbrella terms for the south of Italy.

The scholar's thesis, put simply, is that centuries of feudal rule in the south created a lasting, impermeable environment of institutional exploitation and dependence, making southerners subjects, not citizens, and preventing good government from taking root. Poverty alone doesn't create an uncivic environment, asserts Putnam, who cites examples of altruistic behavior in an Ibo village in Nigeria, among peasants in Java, and in Mexico City. But Putnam can't find what he terms "social trust" throughout all of southern Italy.

The sweeping deterministic logic of *Making Democracy Work*, a popular college textbook that won an award from the National Academy of Public Administration, relegates southern Italians to victimhood, declaring them incapable of achieving the virtues of good citizenship found in the civic north. The book generously quotes from *The Moral Basis of a Backward Society*, and in the preface Putnam cites his mentor Banfield for his insights and critiques.

Few academics have disputed Banfield's theories or offered alternative views of southern Italian life. But recently, coinciding with the fortieth anniversary of the publication of *The Moral Basis of a Backward Society*, Filippo Sabetti of McGill University in Canada challenged the sociologist's research by returning to the southern Italian village that Banfield once described. Sabetti is the first North American academic to visit Chiaromonte and reassess, as best he could nearly a half century later, Banfield's fieldwork. Reinterviewing villagers who met Banfield in the mid-1950s and reviewing archival material that documents the social and political structure of Chiaromonte, Sabetti proposes that town life may have been richer than Banfield had understood. The village, despite operating within an economic system that paid peasants a pittance for working land owned by the rich, had a long history of supporting voluntary community organizations, such as mutual aid societies, lay congregations, and rural cooperatives. The villagers Sabetti interviewed who had met Banfield or had read his work saw the portrait as a "caricature" of life in Chiaromonte, and were "puzzled as to why outsiders, including people in America, have taken Banfield's account so seriously."

Sabetti counters the idea that the peasants were "prisoners of their family-centered ethos." "If the Chiaromontesi at the time of Banfield's fieldwork were indeed 'prisoners,' they were prisoners more of the rules that governed their agricultural and communal activities than of their culture or ethos." The real problem with Banfield's work, suggests Sabetti, is that he never considered whether the villagers could have been "moral familists," trapped inside an exclusionary system and working as best they could to help their families survive the paradox of southern Italy's pastoral yet infertile land.

Amoral familism. Moral familism. The black-and-white symbols of this sociologese sway back and forth, slowly, heavily, and I imagine a cloaked man with fingers long and spindly pointing to a future in the New World, determined by the space between the tiny letter *a:* amoral family, a moral family. To follow Banfield's logic, members of my grandparents' village of Picerno, several hours north of Chiaromonte, were locked into the same system of land tenure that guaranteed their indigence, and would have adopted the selfish impulse to protect their family, acting amorally toward anyone outside the nuclear unit. When my grandparents left Italy, they were barely older than teenagers, poor and hungry, hardly capable of absorbing the value system of the new land they were entering.

Do I bear the atavistic traits of my ancestors? Was my father raised by a tribe of "amoral familists" in New Jersey, and did he inherit their fatalism and pass it along to all of us? The notion of being raised by amoral familists seems absurd, a social experiment like the scientist's taming of the savage forest boy that Truffaut presented in *The Wild Child*. Yet I still hear the echo of my mother's voice: "Trust only the family," she would say. "Blood is thicker than water." Perhaps Banfield's work resonates so strongly in my mind because my parents did act as familists, although I'd like to think the pendulum swung right and we were on its moral side.

The words "Trust only the family" sound like a bad parody, conjuring the vision of a tiny Italian woman shaped like a barrel who repeated old wives' tales and inflicted the evil eye on innocent suspects. My mother, who laughed at *malocchio*, or *maloyke* in her dialect, tried hard to be modern (or "with it," as she would say) while still paying deference to the values of her parents. But modernism escaped her; she made only a few friends outside a small circle of neighbors, and rarely socialized, more comfortable in her housedress sipping a cup of coffee and munching *taralli*, southern Italian biscuits, than joining the ladies who lunched at Lord & Taylor. As we grew older, my mother twisted the notion of family to its most exclusionary construct, our tiny nuclear unit. Yet I believe her words, "Trust only the family," were formed not by some inescapable southern Italian character trait but because my family suffered a deep disillusionment with, and were defeated by, the American institutions they confronted daily. That the nineteenth-century disappointment of my Lucanian grandparents crossed well into the twentieth century of my own family attests to the extraordinary difficulty of acculturation and the arduous journey of escaping poverty.

When people feel trapped within a system, survival instincts take hold, even if such instincts build walls that can take several generations to tear down. My family situation was far different from that of our ancestors, who lived a meager existence on barely arable land. But a basic premise of communal citizenship—the ability to trust and work with institutions, an act of faith foreign to the peasantry—was impaired by our own turn of fate. My parents' first son, Henry, was born mentally retarded in 1946. The resources available to them and to him were limited and disappointing, spinning us closer together in the intricate web of family. Family saves, family shackles, was the dualism I confronted as a child, oppositions that I perhaps felt more intensely than others because my sibling with his special needs never received appropriate help.

My parents chose to live in the sameness of suburbia with a boy who embodied difference, in itself an act of courage. They soon discovered that the institutions they had been taught to trust, the church and the school, would betray their sense of morality. My mother often repeated the story of fighting for Henry to receive his first Holy Communion, and suffering the humiliation of watching the priest mock him in front of other children when he took the host. The paper wafer hung on his tongue for a few interminable seconds, prompting the priest to announce harshly, "Stick your tongue in." My mother had no doubt that his tone, heard several rows back, was a reprimand, not instruction. Several years later, another priest refused to admit Henry to confirmation training—no room at the inn for leftover children of God—and my mother begged an outsider in the Church hierarchy, a nun, to sneak him into a class. These two sacraments—the declaration of faith and right of passage into adulthood in the Catholic Church—were received under a veil of embarrassment and exclusion.

After both incidents my mother implicitly understood that her maternal instincts offered the only protection. Community involvement was suspect; both Henry and the family could be mocked, and her reaction to the incident was a harbinger of the closed-minded decision she would make: keep Henry's ties to the outside world minimal. My middle brother, Bob, and I had to set out on our own during the day and amuse ourselves at night, providing me with the freedom to create a small, confined world out of reach of the parental eye. My mother's energy would be devoted to taking care of Henry.

I knew my father as a quiet man who respected and did not challenge authority. Yet my mother tells me that my father had tried to get Henry better treatment in school, but that both father and son were shamed into defeat. My parents moved to Short Hills when Henry was thirteen, which meant that my brother would go to Millburn Junior High School, the same school system in which my father had been enrolled. Yet Henry's "special class"—as a child I intuitively understood the definition of "special" as something peculiar, not extraordinary—had little individual training for young people with mental difficulties. Rather, in the Darwinian social scheme of higher education at the time, the special class cleaned up after the normal kids. When my father found out that his son's class collected garbage on the grounds each day, he called the teacher to complain. Henry hadn't been sent to school to bag someone else's trash.

Okay, the teacher replied, Henry would be exempt from the garbage pickup. The next day Henry sat alone while his classmates continued their scavenger hunt, and that afternoon the special class received a special treat, a steaming cup of hot chocolate. The sweet aroma filling the cups, the smooth taste that lingered on each tongue and swished down each throat, eluded him; the teacher announced to the class that Henry would be having no hot chocolate because he, unlike the others, hadn't done his civic duty. Frustrated, humiliated, he came home to the protection of the family, and eventually dropped out of school.

Family as sole protector had its own damaging limitations, for Henry and the rest of us. I had to learn from an early age how to manage my fright in the face of my brother's explosive outbursts. Our fear of—no, fear is not strong enough—our terror of Henry's volatile temper dictated family life. As my brother's shouts filled the room, menacing and threatening, I frenetically ran circles around the dining room table. Sometimes the outbursts came in the wake of incidents in which he had been publicly humiliated; other times they came unexpectedly, like a spray of summer hail. The anger grew with each passing year, as he watched others achieve goals that he could not—driving a car, keeping a job, marriage and family. With nowhere else to go, I ran endless laps around the oval parameter, exhausted by my own fear. We were alone, my family, trying to solve problems far beyond the reach of our abilities, substituting a stoic sense of duty for outside expertise.

We may have acted as "familists"; certainly we were outsiders discouraged from participating in an idealistic vision of American citizenship, especially when our family member was acknowledged as a public burden. If church and school authorities dictated how people were supposed to behave, the powerless had to find a place for themselves within those limits.

As early as the first grade, I was described by a teacher as unable to come out of my shell, and as an adolescent my shyness continued to confine me to the periphery of school social life. My inability to fit in was compounded by the peculiarity of our household, my brother's condition, the family leviathan, and the fact that Italian-Americans were a tiny minority in our town. When my junior high school teacher asked if I spoke English, I was left feeling completely alone, out of sync with the routine communication of daily life. My parents weren't there to defend me; I couldn't expect my father to phone the school and complain about the teacher's insensitivity to the vowels in my name. By the time I was an adolescent they had waged enough battles on behalf of my brother.

In Banfield's stilted terminology, my parents showed an "absence of both communal and voluntary collective action." My mother never joined the PTA, like most other women on our block, because she was exhausted by family obligations and embarrassed by her lack of a college degree. While my father did join the Church's Holy Name Society, he was its quiet secretary, a Bartleby the Scrivener, silently recording notes until he preferred not to and was voted out of office. My parents had once tried, when they were younger and less bruised, to assert their authority, to create the appropriate synergy between parent and teacher, parishioner and priest, but the system trounced them and they retreated to the safety of home. My mother questioned who there was left to trust, and her answer was as dark as the peasant's. After many years of failing to find a place for her son in the mainstream, she withdrew, a weary acknowledgment of limitation and defeat.

TODAY MY THOUGHTS ABOUT family appear in recurring dreams, snapshots as obvious to the eye as the simple shapes of a child's puzzle. The film replays the first time I leave home to attend college, my entrance to an independent life. In each dream I reach the same point of conflict: I am supposed to return to school but my attachment to my family makes it difficult to leave; we must have lunch and dinner together, the binding nourishment of Italian life. My bulky powder blue Samsonite luggage sits on the train platform awaiting the thrust of the arriving Amtrak car but I cannot move myself from Newark, New Jersey, to Washington, D.C. My dreams run counter to my own life decisions to walk out the door, but I have never been able to make an adult choice without feeling that I have left my family further behind.

My feelings of attachment may fit the sociologists' distinction between the American ethic of "self-advancement" versus the Italian value of "family advancement." Explanations like these, however, diminish the role of the Italian past in my life, suggesting a superior American value system and assuming that a family-centered culture is less healthy than an individualistic one. And they fail to account for the complicated dynamics of family life. Part of my mother wanted me by her side, but she sent me off to a college hundreds of miles away; in fact, she inverted the stereotype of the typical Italian mother, preferring that her daughter pursue a career than get married and have a family.

Banfield's notion that American citizens act collectively to advance community welfare is also dated and quaint in an age when people distrust government and fierce personal interests rule; by recent standards, Italian-Americans, who have learned to use the tools of assimilation like all other nineteenth-century immigrant groups, behave as "American" as anyone else. (Robert Putnam's new book, *Bowling Alone*, chronicles the increasing alienation that Americans have felt since the 1960s.) A footnote in *Making Democracy Work* suggests that a "complete exit from this infernal social setting" of southern Italy is one means of escaping the fate of the amoral familist. Perhaps Putnam believes that the great civic traditions of Anglo-Saxon society have saved Italian-Americans, or at least some of us, from our predetermined destiny as amoral familists.

After reading both men, I was reminded of Virginia Woolf's

famous attack on the works of Arnold Bennett, John Galsworthy, and H. G. Wells, and how years later her acquaintance Isaiah Berlin would use Woolf's manifesto for a new fiction designed to make a broader political point. These men were "blind materialists," Berlin wrote, "who did not begin to understand what it is that life truly consists of, who mistook its outer accidents, the unimportant aspects which lie outside the individual soul—the so-called social, economic, political realities—for that which alone is genuine, the individual experience, the specific relation of individuals to one another, the colours, smells, tastes, sounds, and movements, the jealousies, loves, hatreds, passions, the rare flashes of insight, the transforming moments, the ordinary day-to-day succession of private data which constitute all there is—which are reality."

Where is the truth to our history? I've come to see the Banfields and Putnams of the world as the scholarly version of the high school friend who called me the "smelly Italian girl." Each imposed his or her value system on my culture by using a biased lexicon or vernacular: southern Italians are amoral/uncivic/smelly.

Is it possible for Italian-Americans to see the past through a different lens, uncolored by the preconceptions and political agendas of others—but also freed from a false romanticism? Why do so many Italian-Americans insist on hearing only "nice stories" about our heritage when the majority of our ancestors came from a land plagued by misery and sadness—in modern language, a dysfunctional past? Perhaps the pace of this ethnic group's assimilation, which has been quicker than that of darker-skinned "others" like Latinos and African-Americans, has led to an abandonment of the kind of acute intellectual reflection that these groups have engaged in as they attempt to understand their relationship to the past and their place within the larger culture.

Maybe third- and fourth-generation Italian-Americans will have the distance to interpret the reels of the past, and, unconstrained by the need to pretty up the story, can begin to unravel the many layers that compose an individual life.

As I continue to see the Italian-American past portrayed in coffee-table and recipe books, watch hagiographic documentaries about the immigrant struggle, and read successive generations of Harvard scholars pejoratively define Italian-American culture, I struggle to accept my own version of Italian spirits and their influence on me. Neither enduring the immigrants' hardships nor experiencing their offsprings' desire for acceptance during a time in which Italy was the enemy, I travel a more leisurely route, attempting to sort out the artifacts of American culture said to be Italian. But still the picture is half complete. While the cultural biases here in America are daunting, likewise difficult to navigate is the serpentine path that separates northern and southern Italians.

Clothes

AT THE CORNER OF Madison Avenue and Sixty-eighth Street stand a pair of buildings that once told the story of contemporary fashion through the vision of two Italians, one born in the genteel "civic" north, the other from the rugged "uncivic" south of Italy. In a simpler time perhaps, before the designer Giorgio Armani moved into his colossal flagship store a few blocks away, before Gianni Versace opened his own fashion palace on Fifth Avenue and ultimately became a household name because of his brutal murder, these two competed for customers, staking out like feuding neighbors their starkly different stylistic territory. The pull and tug of these men, archrivals, master weavers of myth, reminds me of my youth and the role that clothes played in our household. Not that we knew anything about haute couture when I was growing up. But we did know something about good taste and bad taste.

Above the red brick entrance to the old Armani boutique is a large airy window in the shape of an arch; it resembles a church window, simple and Protestant, a fitting image for the northern Italian often thought of as the high priest of Milanese fashion. To wear the name Giorgio Armani is to bear an imprimatur of luxury and distinction. To enter an Armani shop is to step into the land of taste, a subdued world where shades of beige quietly rule, and in their elegance and beauty conquer.

Next door, the charcoal gray Versace boutique is embellished with sixteen faux Corinthian columns, each crowned with a silver cornice. The Versace window display, always a kaleidoscope of colors, one spring season featured mannequins draped in bright orange, accessorized with matching-color patent leather bags and shiny spike-heeled shoes; these were fiery warriors next to Armani's neutral goddesses. Showy gewgaws adorned the clothes inside; Versace's gold Medusa-head emblem fastens belts, buttons sweaters, and clamps purses shut.

Gianni Versace made an extraordinary career for himself by breaking the rules of fashion, openly defying what Roland Barthes called the "taboo of an aesthetic order," tweaking the tasteful upturned nose of Armani clothes. As Barthes explained in his book *The Fashion System,* "the structural definition of bad taste is linked to this variant: vestimentary depreciation most often occurs through a profusion of elements, accessories and jewels." Or as *Vogue* editor in chief Anna Wintour once put it: "Versace was always sort of the 'mistress' to Armani's wife."

Armani was said to have grumbled about the direction of Italian fashion led by Versace, a trend that some of their colleagues playfully labeled "the good taste of bad taste." But it would be impossible to understand the source of the Armani-Versace rivalry without recognizing that the style of both designers was derived in part from the contradictory outlook of a country deeply divided by class.

MY GUARDIANS OF FASHION, my mother and my aunt, would never have made a Versace-like mistake. They would not have worn a bright orange dress with matching patent leather sandals or overdecorated sweaters, sure signs of lower-class Italian-American taste. I would become their model, and they would dress me to look delicate, refined, a picture of good taste.

For many years, my mother and my aunt divided up the duty of dressing me. My aunt took the first decade, my mother watched over the next two. My aunt, a widow in her forties, lived alone in a small apartment and spent most of her paycheck from a clerical job at Western Electric on clothes for herself. She also delighted in dressing her brother's child, and my earliest clothes memories are a swirl of pastels: baby pink, blue, and yellow, the colors of my Easter suits, light wools that hung tentatively on my tiny body, as if the sheep were surprised by the tender age of their new home. Dresses, jackets, skirts, and blouses. Soft cottons, cool wools, cuddly bouclés.

My closet filled with clothes allowed me to dress up and to make believe, replacing toys as the child's suspension bridge into the land of wonder, providing me with a passageway to an imaginary, grown-up world. I was much more preoccupied with the interchangeable satin ribbons that accessorized my new straw hat than dolling up a Barbie, and I deliberated with great care over what color to wear each week. I would carry my head high as I walked into church on Sundays, with a touch of forest green or burgundy wrapped above the brim to accent a navy coat.

Early on I learned about the age barrier to dressing for success. In kindergarten, I carried home a handwritten note from my teacher informing my mother that I was inappropriately dressed; my clothes were too good for a five-year-old who spent half of her day crawling and napping on a floor mat. Because girls were not allowed to wear pants, I needed play dresses, but a less fancy outfit (a housedress?) could never fit my aunt's image of what I should look like at school. The dresses were so pretty that we ignored the teacher's comment and I learned to kneel on the floor like a Japanese princess at tea.

Each fashion season, my aunt would buy me dresses and colorful tights to match and bring them to our house, except on special occasions, like the week before Easter, when she would take me shopping and out to lunch at her favorite department store, Haynes in Newark, New Jersey. I would sit in the plain Haynes lounge with its faded wallpaper and wait for a gray-haired waitress to deliver my tuna fish melt, all of which seemed resplendent to me. Afterward, we would shop.

"I like this one," I'd say with an eight-year-old's authority, and point to a two-piece electric yellow knit. My aunt let me try it on, along with several others, but she had already chosen my Easter dress. The outfit I picked out looked "cheesy," she said. I assumed she meant it bore a color resemblance to Cheddar cheese, and tried to convince myself that her choice was better than mine.

My mother trusted my aunt to buy me clothes, but I could never tell how much she liked her sister-in-law's taste, although she always accepted the gifts with thanks and praise. The two women looked very different, my mother with her salt-and-pepper short-cropped hair and old cotton housedresses, and my aunt, who wore her dyed red hair in a flip and always came to visit us in a new outfit. My mother's hands were red and chafed from the soapy water she used to clean the dishes and floor each day; my aunt's fingernails were painted in creamy ivory, and she stared at them often, although I never knew whether she was admiring their luster or mourning the absence of the wedding band she once wore. While my mother envied my aunt's freedom to pamper herself, I think she always believed that her own taste was finer, with her eye for simple, elegant cuts. Yet she was raising three children and my father's wallet was emptier. My mother did understand the essential role that clothes could play in fashioning a look and a life of refinement and beauty. She may have had a limited wardrobe, but she had much greater expectations for her daughter.

I can recall best one outfit of my mother's: a khaki-colored suit worn with either a plain black or white scoop-necked cotton shirt. She believed in buying "one nice thing," a finely made suit that could be used many times, rather than several cheaper items. Minimalism guided her choices because she feared excess, afraid as she was of looking Italian-American, or *gavone* (pronounced "gah-vone"). *Gavone*, which we used as both adjective and noun, was southern Italian dialect derived from the Italian word *cafone*, or ignorant person. The word meant to us—if one can ever interpret precisely the variable nuances of dialect—low-class. (I didn't realize until years later that *cafone* was the label northern Italians used to mock poor southerners.) *Gavone* outfits combined a sexiness and tackiness that left me awestruck in their excessive splendor.

I had an early encounter with this look as a child at a cocktail party my parents gave prior to a church event. One relative entered our house wearing a tight orange cardigan with a plunging V-neck, a gold cross that dangled between her breasts, clinging black pants, and high-heeled sandals. "That's quite a sweater," my mother laughed nervously, and she did seem to like the cardigan despite its audaciousness. I stood close to this relative for most of the evening, impressed by her full figure, admiring the way her body looked, but disturbed that she had worn this outfit to a gathering attended by a priest. She had Gianni Versace in her bones before the designer ever sold his first pair of skintight pants.

Italian-American clothes were colorful and baroque, often worn by women with jet black hair piled high on the head: tops in turquoise, chartreuse, shocking pink, purple, and coral (an especially popular color at weddings) and clashing pants; dresses dripping with brocades; gold shoes. Like any adolescent who follows fashion trends as if they were the Holy Grail, for years I amused myself flipping through magazines trying to determine that fine line between *gavone* and chic. Beautiful models wore raging reds, shocking pinks, and deep purples, yet those same colors could create that over-the-top Italian-American look. How would I know if I was *gavone* or chic?

Today it amuses me when a design that fits my childhood image of Italian-American taste is labeled haute couture. Yet many of the top designers are Italian, some came from the poorest regions of southern Italy, and how else is fashion created but from memory, the palette of colors, textures, and objects appropriated from one's youth? Over a half century ago, the linguist Edward Sapir wrote, "The chief difficulty of understanding fashion in its apparent vagaries is the lack of exact knowledge of the unconscious symbolisms attaching to forms, colors, textures, postures and other expressive elements of a given culture."

CLOTHES CONJURED FOR ME the dual demons of pride and embarrassment, of joy and fear. Like any girl, I loved dressing up, but at five, after being told about the note from my teacher, I had a vague feeling that my clothes were inappropriate, that there was too much effort spent in trying to make me look right, putting me in dresses when play clothes would do. And I never was allowed to forget the value of good clothes, which made it hard to act like a child.

My aunt once bought me a pair of royal blue tights that matched a cotton dress, and I put the gift aside, awaiting the perfect spring day to wear them. When I finally deemed my legs ready for this swathe of blue, I tripped that day during recess and tore a hole at the knee, which protruded beneath the fabric like a gibbous moon. I wept the rest of the afternoon, anticipating a reprise of my mother's angry, oft-repeated lecture: "You don't deserve good clothes." (Who deserves good clothes? People who can afford to tear them? Children who don't fall down when they play?)

Soon I began to dislike the way clothes looked on me because my once skinny body had grown plump. My normally quiet father grew talkative about the issue of my weight. He was fearful that his daughter would suffer the sad fate of his secretary, who had been engaged to a doctor but had, after ballooning in size, ended up marrying a mozzarella maker. While I was eating vanilla ice cream drenched in Hershey's syrup and topped with Reddi Wip, he muttered that I was becoming "as fat as a house," perhaps envisioning my future of kneading and tossing dough for a demanding husband in a full apron stained with milky curds.

By the time I reached the age of ten or eleven, my aunt had grown tired of buying clothes for me, showing up with less and less until she stopped altogether. A chubby girl wasn't as fun to dress, and buying clothes had become a costlier proposition. My aunt explained that an adolescent was too difficult to shop for, and she would wait until I became "a perfect size ten." I believed her, having no sense of the little deceits adults commit when they trap themselves in a box and, upon grasping its dimensions and limitations, desperately wish to escape.

"When you're a perfect ten [the size that she wore], I'll know how to shop for you," my aunt repeated. Her explanation had the cadence of a lullaby, pacifying my anxieties about my body and promising a better future. So I naïvely dreamed of turning into a lady, becoming the "perfect ten," pleasing my elders, and awakening a few years later to walk down the runway of my aunt's taste and charge card.

Because clothes played such a large part in my mother's anxieties about becoming an American, I'm sure that her mixed feelings about leaving my early dressing to my aunt were compounded by her own fear of having to shop for me. "Your sister spoiled her. She got used to good things," my mother would say to my father, who knew that there was no acceptable answer.

"And now we have to buy her nice clothes," she'd conclude to the air. My mother understood that the choice of what to wear could allow you to be something you are not, that fabric and style could transcend class labels, providing the essential threads for a Pygmalion tale. My aunt had the perfect arrangement, according to my mother's fantasy of the single woman's life: she spent very little money on housing, living in a small apartment in an urban area of New Jersey; her success was measured by the clothes she wore in the world.

My mother's sensitivity to the transformative power of clothes was part and parcel of her second-generation instinct to assimilate, and like most children of immigrants, she juggled the difficulties of leaving the Old World to adapt to the New. While she loved her parents, they spoke with a heavy accent and looked like Italian immigrants. Her responsibility to act like a dutiful daughter and her desire to adopt the image of an American suburban housewife and mother could be mutually exclusive, and she lacked the confidence—or the ability to create the *bella figura*—needed to pull off the latter. In trying to abandon the stereotype of the Italian—the greaseball, the *gavone*—mixed messages abounded in our household. My mother wanted to maintain traditions, keep the spirit of our humble origins, but at the same time reject a look that we labeled lower-class.

If ancestry could be masked in the weave of a classic style, then her daughter, educated and well dressed, could achieve dreams beyond my mother's reach. But clothes choices need validation, and my mother, isolated and alone in our house, was ill at ease shopping in a department store. "I don't trust my taste," she said, explaining that she envied women who always knew what they wanted. She would dither and nervously wander among the racks, and ultimately feel helpless until she found a saleswoman to affirm the choices in her hand.

My mother had one story about clothes that she repeated like a Scheherazade tale, hoping its message could redeem a lost part of herself. The time was several years before her marriage, those strange days of contained independence for a young woman engaged to an army officer stationed in Europe; the place, a cozy sweater shop far from the horrors her fiancé was facing. There the manager put my mother in charge of selecting the finest sweaters delivered to his shop. He would seek her opinion and showcase the cottons and wools that she had picked; always, she said, he would compliment her choices. The store gave my mother a place to nurture an identity that thrived on the notion of possessing good taste.

The story sadly reminded me of her brief working life, stopped short by marriage and children. As a teenager I wanted to say, "What do you care what that stupid man thought anyway? Why does his judgment, not yours, mean that you have good taste?" But I knew better than to respond. The image of those pretty sweaters comforted my mother like a blanket of luxurious wool during years of servitude to a husband of immeasurable silences and children who grew old too soon.

Children never want to see their parents' youthful possibilities, and perhaps that was the reason why I refused to imagine this scene in the sweater shop. I understood and accepted her fashion advice as a mother's advice, a gauge that set limits to the child's limitless wants. But as a daughter, I didn't think about her youthful investment, how she looked in clothes before she was married, the persona she adapted by wearing what she chose, and, most unimaginably, how men saw what covered her body. In her married life, my mother abandoned clothes that she may have chosen in that sweater shop, clothes that could heighten her dark-haired allure. I, too, agreed with her choices. Her judgment would mute my love of the bright and bold.

TODAY FASHION DESIGNERS ARE celebrities; television, magazines, and movies inform us about the objects and memories that have influenced the men and women who dress the supermodels and the stars. Miuccia Prada, an Italian designer made famous in America after the actress Uma Thurman wore a Prada dress to the 1995 Academy Awards, told a television interviewer that the mottled plastic links she used for handles on her leather bags were inspired by the tortoiseshells her father collected when she was a child. *Unzipped,* a documentary about Isaac Mizrahi, included old footage of the designer's mother clomping in flowered mules. Mizrahi explained that his mother's 1950s footwear would resurface years later in his designs.

Gianni Versace was the fashion world's great success story. Born the son of a dressmaker from Reggio di Calabria, by the time of his death he had reportedly built an $800 million empire. He was inspired by, and dressed, many muses, including a vampy Madonna, a curvaceous Elizabeth Hurley, and a royally sensual Princess Di. Versace left southern Italy by the age of twenty to design costumes for the theater, and early on in his career he pronounced his clear differences with the reigning king of Italian fashion, Giorgio Armani.

I looked up what the *New York Times* fashion pages had said about both men over the years: "The Armani style is classic and subdued, as opposed to Versace's more flamboyant, obviously sexy look."

"And they had Giorgio Armani on one hand to take care of good practical, classic daytime fashion, and Gianni Versace on the other to cast the die for sexy clothes."

"Nothing interfered with the well-bred look. An occasional pink, mauve or red tweed suit varied the parade of Armani neutrals. . . . [Versace is] known for his flashy colors and complex prints. . . . Later came stinging chartreuse and acid yellow colors along with stretch jump suits in curving wrought-iron prints."

If clothes function simultaneously, as Roland Barthes argued, as the body's "substitute and mask," designers are the conjurers behind the curtain, continually reinventing looks for the consumer, along with their own images. Versace's life suggests such wizardry. The designer incorporated and exploited fame with such aplomb that in his last fashion book, *Rock and Royalty*, he showcased a picture of his family on the page opposite an official portrait of Princess Diana with her sons, suggesting that he, along with sister Donatella and brother Santo, were scions of royal Italian blood.

In a *New Yorker* profile published shortly after Versace's death, the writer Andrea Lee offered accounts of Versace's past that were as varied as his color palette. Versace described to Lee what it was like to grow up in the "romantic atmosphere of a rich bourgeois family: Father was a businessman who loved opera and literature; Mother was the glamorous, free-spirited proprietress of an important dressmaking atelier."

In a *New York Times* article he remarked, "When you are born in a place and there is beauty all around, a Roman bath, a Greek remain, you cannot help but be influenced by the classical past." Versace's descriptions of Reggio di Calabria served to polish the shabby image of the Italian boot, reclaiming its stature as the land of Greek antiquity where Pythagoras dreamed and poets honored Scylla and Charybdis, not the dreary villages plagued by *la miseria*, the abounding poverty that defines so much of the south.

The Versace Italian myth became emblazoned in stone, a fitting tribute to a man who chose the Medusa head as his fashion logo: the King of Fashion wanted his family business to be run like the Medicis, he once said. He was about "class, not mass," a newspaper columnist wrote. Richard Martin, curator of the Costume Institute at the Metropolitan Museum of Art, described Versace: "To say that he lives like a prince is not to say merely that he lives affluently, but that he is a modernized version of the Renaissance tradition of the learned, artistically discriminating cultural leader." The death of this prince for the nineties was eclipsed only by that of a real princess the following month.

Later in the *New Yorker* profile, Lee offered a revised version of the Versace family history. A sportswear designer who had known Versace for decades commented, "There was no rich background, no grand, high-fashion atelier. They were a simple family: the father sold appliances, and the mother made dresses in her little shop. It was a *merceria-abbigliamento* [a small clothing shop that also sells buttons and accessories] and its name, if I recall, was Vogue. The rest is fantasy."

While the blue-eyed Giorgio Armani, born in Piacenza, an hour away from Milan, grew up surrounded by upper-class Italian style, the nearest capitals for the young Versace would have been Naples, hundreds of miles north, and Palermo, farther south, both considered by northerners to be embarrassments of corruption and decay, and, until designers like Gianni Versace and Dolce & Gabbana came on the scene, the last places to look for inspiration to dress the elegant fashion consumer.

Versace was surrounded by the tastes of southern Italy. It is the taste of poor and working-class people; it is Barthes's "profusion of elements," the composition of bad taste. Bright Mediterranean colors, the earthy sensuality of peasants, the excessive pageantry of the religious south, and a baroque style that rejected simplicity as a metaphor for the Teutonic, northern way of life were images a young Versace would have internalized.

I was struck by English novelist George Gissing's recollection of the peasant women he encountered in Calabria in his 1901 travel book on southern Italy, *By the Ionian Sea*, because the writer's descriptions fit the look of an early Versace runway model: "The women wore a very striking costume: a short petticoat of scarlet, much embroidered, and over it a blue skirt, rolled up in front and gathered in a sort of knot behind the waist; a bodice adorned with needlework and metal; elaborate glistening head-gear, and bare feet."

"What is Versace all about?" a *New York Times* fashion writer asked nearly a century later. "Quite simply, a lot. Of everything. Full-blast prints. All-out beadwork. Poufs and big, floating skirts (the underwiring is sometimes so wide it looks as if a curtain fell over a bicycle)."

The *gavone* Italian-American look had to have originated in the tastes of southern Italy, carried from one generation to the next. As Gianni Versace rose to the highest echelons of the fashion world, he blotted out his rustic past but achieved success by using attributes of peasant style in his designs.

The nineteenth-century sociologist Georg Simmel, in his essay "Fashion," offered an argument about the origins of taste known as the "trickle-down theory" of style. Simmel suggested that the upper classes control trends and styles by choosing certain types of clothes which eventually become popular with the masses, and which will be imitated by them.

"Just as soon as the lower classes begin to copy their style," he writes, "thereby crossing the line of demarcation the upper classes have drawn and destroying the uniformity of their coherence, the upper classes turn away from this style and adopt a new one, which in its turn differentiates them from the masses; and the game goes merrily on." In the last century, Simmel's theory has been embraced, abandoned, revised, and defended again. But if elements of the essay's truth still exist, the theory reverses itself when applied to the work of the ethnic designer. Certainly the upper classes no longer control taste. The influence of street fashion, from hooded sweatshirts to rubber bangle bracelets, has been one of the most significant trends in design, and the appropriation of the street look by haute couture is an overt, forceful statement.

The inspiration, however, for many of Gianni Versace's designs, the use of bright, clashing colors, the passion for the gaudily ornate, is quite different from street fashion's rebellious origins. The excessive elements often found in working-class taste may be the result of trying to copy the rich, and overcompensating. Versace inverted the Simmel theory: he allowed the lower class to influence and change upper-class fashion.

Fashion writers often described Versace as subversive, yet to me his styles always felt familiar, vaguely comforting, coming from roots that I know. If fashion has historically been a way to enhance and solidify social status—at least, that's what we hoped for in our household—Versace changed the game: he internalized the taste of the poor, drawing on the influences of southern Italy to create a multimillion-dollar empire. Perhaps that's the subversion, the fact that he had turned haute couture on its head with designs that might be called *basse* couture.

IN THE 1970S, THE only designers my mother and I knew were those who mass-marketed clothes, attaching their fussy initials to T-shirts, ties, and sheets. My mother, however, could have used some Armani-like help now that my aunt had closed her chapter in my fashion story. With my mother in charge of my wardrobe, she had to ensure that her daughter wouldn't look *gavone*. Luckily, she had a convenient means of protection: we lived within walking distance of a branch of Saks Fifth Avenue. Once my mother decided that we would shop at Saks, I'm sure she also experienced the satisfaction of one-upping my aunt. Haynes was a middle-class New Jersey store; Saks symbolized the epitome of upper-crust taste.

My mother still knew that there were mistakes to be made among the assorted racks of the preteen department, and she was worried about having the time to shop for me because she worked as a secretary to help pay college tuition bills for my brother Bob. She befriended an elderly woman named Mrs. Smith who managed the preteen department, and my mother asked her to be in charge of shopping for my clothes. We worked out an arrangement: I would walk to Saks after school carrying my mother's charge card, and would find Mrs. Smith. Because children usually adapt to the circumstances they're presented with, it never struck me as odd that my mother didn't take me shopping; her excuses about time pressures seemed to make sense.

Mrs. Smith, a small woman with powder white hair and a face mapped with wrinkles, might have been more comfortable pointing a ruler at a blackboard filled with English grammar than lifting plastic hangers and prodding me toward the dressing room, which she did as we solemnly approached each fitting. I was uncomfortable with this little woman standing next to me while I undressed, nodding, judging, surveying my body from head to toe, but my mother seemed to have supreme confidence in her choice of Mrs. Smith as the new designee to mold my fashion taste. It was as if she had found the perfect headmistress and had just enrolled me in boarding school at Saks.

The few times a year that I bought school clothes became a chore because I now had to please Mrs. Smith as well as my mother, and as an adolescent I had exuberant taste, preferring crayon-box colors (an incipient Versaceite?) to the muted shades my mother had in mind. And we made a few mistakes, Mrs. Smith and I, with some major purchases, like the winter coat debacle. We picked out a long, powder blue coat with a curly white wool collar and two large pockets embroidered in iridescent swirls of pink, blue, and purple that resembled a butterfly fluttering through a bad trip. Mrs. Smith thought it was marvelous, this coat dubbed "the Butterfly" by my brother Bob. My mother hated it, but what could she say—Mrs. Smith had helped choose the woolly wonder and she couldn't insult her taste. Although I insisted I loved the coat, after two winter seasons I began to feel like a ripe caterpillar that wanted to touch the sky but forever was a chrysalis trapped inside its neon cocoon.

WALKING INTO THE VERSACE boutique, I feel relaxed and amused. I pass the glossy vinyl pants and dazzling striped tops, and pick up a scanty red shift decorated with three-inch metal zippers at the chest and longer zippers that serve as front pockets. The shift looks like a racy version of the housedresses my mother wore, except it's thirteen hundred dollars. I can imagine older women buying the cashmere sweaters in argyle pastels with gold lamé running through the wool, crowned with Medusa-head buttons. I notice the sharp stare of a saleswoman; I am an intruder with no intention to buy, and feel superior rejecting overdone, overpriced clothes.

In the Armani shop, I am tense looking at clothes that I find beautiful, racks of long beige jackets and slim-cut pants as delicately varied in shade as grains of sand, and gauzy blouses that move effortlessly, like a calm breeze. I feel out of place, self-conscious; I am among people with whom I don't belong, next to clothes that I cannot afford. His is a fairy-tale world of clothes, a kingdom that I could pretend to live in as a child, and still long for as an adult.

The styles of these two men were the yin and yang of my youth: clothes could make you look southern Italian or Anglo-Saxon, extravagant or refined, sexy or powerful. In choosing either style, I had something to lose.

FOR MY MOM AND ME, clothes were the purest comfort. Clothes formed one of our strongest and, for a time, it seemed, least threatening bonds, giving us a lasting topic of conversation, a point of mutual interest compared to schoolwork, which failed to hold my mother's attention, or cooking, which was solely her domain, her short body and sturdy legs positioned by the electric stove, where she stirred and I sat a few feet away. We could talk about clothes as we watched TV, discussing the latest styles or reminiscing about memorable looks, like the tight black leggings that Mary Tyler Moore wore on "The Dick Van Dyke Show" long before anyone else.

My mother didn't realize that when she cut the umbilical cord so young, teaching me the importance of fashion and yet using intermediaries to send me out in style, there would be a natural yet unforeseen result. I would develop my own taste, which I would use to place myself in the world. The rift between us grew after I left home for college.

One summer, my application for a saleswoman's job at our favorite spot, the local Saks, was accepted. About a month into my summer job, the personnel director stopped by my department to tell me about a "Fashion Board" for college students that I might like to join, which would include an end-of-the-summer fashion show. She told me to see a woman named Maureen who was running the board. My conversation with the personnel director led me to believe that I had already been selected, and I didn't realize that Maureen was judging each girl.

The look on Maureen's face when I entered her small corner office in the back of the store told me that my future modeling career was not yet assured. "I'm just not sure you're right for us," she said, looking me up and down and acting as if the "us" were the Ford modeling agency and she were choreographing the next shoot in Milan. I was probably ten pounds heavier than Maureen desired, and I was darker than the rest of the girls I would meet, most of whom had blond or sandy brown hair.

My confidence withered, and I felt like a character out of *The Adventures of Augie March*, a book I quoted often during those years, returning to Bellow's words of wisdom on my dog-eared green index cards attached to a spiral wire. Like Augie, I decided that I was powerless in the face of all those who misunderstand "how you're liked for what you're not, disliked for what you're not, both from error and laziness. The way must be not to care, but in that case you must know how really to care and understand what's pleasing or displeasing in yourself."

Those words, mouthed over and over, were little solace to a youthful ego that shifted between miserable self-pity and angry self-righteousness. Eventually I was accepted to the board; each girl had to submit an essay about fashion, and Maureen, who circled the Saks parking lot in a red Mercedes with a personalized license plate that read "Moo-reen," seemed to enjoy the name-dropping piece that I wrote. The prospect of the fashion show kept my attention during the tedious hours of a sales day. But my head buzzed with alarms from all those years of shopping: Don't look cheesy, don't look *gavone*—you must have good taste. What clothes would my aunt have liked? What would Mrs. Smith have chosen? Would my mother approve?

As the show approached, we were told to choose sporty outfits, except for our last walk down the runway, which called for an elegant dress. I wasn't entirely pleased with the selection of clothes before me, but I picked out checked and solid wool pants and blazers that I could imagine wearing in school. For my last dress I decided to have some fun with a slinky, bright purple silk sheath.

The night of the show, the main floor of Saks was temporarily rearranged for the evening, filled with little wooden folding chairs and bright-colored balloons that surrounded a makeshift catwalk installed between the handbag and blouse departments. The personnel director took aside our group of jittery girls about to face a handful of people and a horde of balloons and gave some last-minute advice: Smile, she said. Look like you're having a good time. And when you're on the runway, dance to the music.

All of us exchanged complaints to forget about the stage fright. We lined up, single file, in the hallway of the dressing rooms, giggling and primping, complimenting each other, forgetting that we had barely exchanged a word during the previous weeks together in the department store. Perhaps because girls are dressed up, and dress up dolls so young, bonding can be simple and pure when zippers and buttons get fastened.

Soon the music played and, following our cue, we began an odd-looking prance, each unsure of how to walk and dance down the runway. Skipping, walking, running, I was through most of my wools and still didn't see my mother, who I knew would be detained by her after-dinner cleanup. By the time I entered the dressing room to slip into my last outfit, the sleeveless purple silk, I had begun to relax. Feeling elegant and happy, I added a little extra jump to my step as I started down the runway. Completing a twirl, I noticed that my mother had arrived; already she looked displeased by what she saw.

Back in the dressing room, I received polite but tepid enthusiasm, with no suggestions of a budding modeling career. My mother and I walked home together, a sullen and silent ten-minute trip. Knowing what was bothering her and in a bald search for approval, I asked how I looked.

As soon as we reached our house, she unleashed her fury: my little dance on the runway was embarrassing. Why wasn't I walking in a sophisticated way? Why had I picked that purple dress? I tried to explain that we were told to dance and look happy, but soon my eyes filled with tears and words poured out of my mouth in a pathetic attempt at self-defense. Screaming in the hallway, I hardly noticed that my mother, seated on our worn blue couch with her head bowed, had started to cry. I was stunned by the rare sight of my mother crying but furious that she had the power to make me feel so awful.

It was dark in the upstairs of our house; my father and brothers were watching television on the floor below, pretending to be oblivious to the mother-and-teenage-daughter battle that raged above them. We screamed into the night without bothering even to turn on a light, as if the darkness could absorb our wounds. I had betrayed my mother's sense of good taste; she had betrayed my hope for approval. I knew the argument was ludicrous, my offense minor, but still I couldn't stop the shouting or the tears. Clothes were supposed to make me accepted, serious, responsible. Instead, I had picked a bright purple sheath and frivolously danced down the runway.

That night the wounds of many years reopened. My mother never had the pleasure of dressing her child, handing over that responsibility first to my aunt and then to a stranger at Saks. That night we shared a mutual anger; we each had a story about the other that we wished we could erase. As I couldn't imagine the sweaters she had chosen that won another man's admiration, she couldn't accept me wearing a close-fitting silk dress that outlined my young body. The purpose of good clothes was to make us Americans, not to heighten our Mediterranean sexuality; to tamper with the power of clothes, to allow them to seduce, could cause an explosion like the one I witnessed that night.

My clothes memories always bring me back to the early moments of painful separation, the night of the fashion show when I watched my mother reduced to tears as she sat on a torn and faded couch. Her hopes had been put into clothes, into the illusion that a beautiful, tasteful dress could provide the wearer with the necessary confidence to meet the world. I'm sure she believed that she could have saved me that night, that another dress would have shaped me into a prettier, better person. If only she hadn't had to rely on others for judgment or for money; if she could have picked out clothes for both of us with the same confidence that she had had in the sweater shop, receiving praise for those luxurious, creamy wools that she alone had chosen.

WHEN I WAS IN my late twenties, my mother continued to walk to Saks several times a month in a faded raincoat, once a handsome purchase from the store, and flat shoes with worn heels. She would pick out clothes for me as soon as they were marked down, proud of the savings. For the first time in my life, my mother actually dressed me, and her shopping lasted until I got married, ending the irreplaceable comfort of my mother taking care of my needs.

Maybe because I no longer lived at home, dressing me proved to be the best connection between us, and she could ensure that in my nascent working life I looked good. And it embarrassed me that I only received compliments on the clothes she had picked out—elegant tailored skirts and jackets, thick cowl-neck sweaters and silk blouses—but never on my own choices. "Let her shop for me," "Give me that jacket when you're tired of it," my friends would say. (What was equally surprising was that I worked at the *Village Voice,* and all the clothes my colleagues liked came from the haut bourgeois Saks.)

Today my wardrobe consists mainly of black and beige, with an occasional touch of bright red. My bland color scheme may be the product of putting on the monochrome mask that many New Yorkers choose to wear, as well as my internal check not to look too Italian-American. I have inherited my mother's taste, and have become even more conservative in my choices, seeking comfort in quiet shades when a little color would serve me well.

"WHO WAS HE?" MY mother asks me on the phone after reports about the Versace murder blare on CNN night after night. "Your brother said his clothes were *gavone.* Is that right?"

I avoided a direct answer, wanting to pay Versace homage with a small tribute, not a sarcastic quip. Afterward, I thought about what Versace had achieved with his look of elegant whimsy. I thought about the endurance of his media legend, how Versace, too, would be liked for what he was not, disliked for what he was not; how we all weave myths in fabric, create a self in the clothes we wear; how my impulse to reject his fanciful palette and Versace's desire to color his background had a similar beginning: the self-consciousness of a southern Italian past. So as I considered my mother's question, I realized that the man who wished to be a Medici was also due a peasant elegy. Yes, his clothes were *gavone*, and the world rightly proclaimed them chic.

Rome

My Piazza Navona can turn up its nose
At poor Piazza di Spagna or St. Peter's Square.
This is no piazza. In many ways
It's more a countryside. Or a stage. Or a fair.

—G. G. BELLI
Rome, February 1, 1883

Fabrizio?" MOANED MY MOTHER. "I'm embarrassed to
tell my friends that my daughter is dating someone called Fabrizio." Nearly a century since her parents Natale and Maria Conte
had stepped foot in America, their granddaughter had to meet a
man whose name had no English equivalent.

"What's wrong with his name?" I snapped back, not admitting that I too disliked it (and so did Fabrizio, a twenty-six-year-old Italian enamored of all things American). The conversation took place after I had returned from a vacation in Rome. I had traveled there regularly since 1981, but at the end of the decade, this trip was different; I had just met a young Roman lawyer and was flush with infatuation.

After returning to New York in mid-fall, I decided to buy an early Christmas present for Fabrizio to keep his presence real. My sixth sense for shopping (don't do *gavone*) sent me to Paul Stuart on Madison Avenue, a more expensive Brooks Brothers, the classic preppy man's store. I went to the scarf department looking for something neither showy nor intimate, and a saleswoman, well dressed amid the box plaids and houndstooth checks, offered to help. She presented me with an array of colors. Touching a soft off-white wool, I buried an instant of fear, realizing that I hardly knew the recipient of my gift.

"Can you describe his taste?" the saleswoman asked, as if detecting my secret terror.

The fabric of the scarf, cut long and wide, draped a man's chest, requiring a bit of self-confidence.

"I'm not certain of his taste," I replied, embarrassed. "He's Italian."

The saleswoman and a middle-aged blonde standing next to me wrapped in layers of wool met eyes, trying to bury my faux pas with a silent stare. They had interpreted my odd comment as an attempt to describe someone, or perhaps ghettoize someone, by his ethnicity, and the Madison Avenue image of an "Italian" was not a person who lives in Italy but the young men from Bensonhurst known as "guidos." I quickly tried to dig myself out.

"Would it be possible to ship this gift to Rome?"

"Oh, he's Your-oh-peean," the saleswoman said gleefully, emphasizing the difference between an Italian and an "Italian" as she stretched out the syllables.

"Europeans love light colors."

The other woman nodded enthusiastically and chimed in, "You should buy him the off-white scarf."

Proud of the cachet of a "Your-oh-peean" boyfriend, I bought the scarf and sent it to Italy. I would learn the hard way that I was in love not with this Roman but with Rome, a city that changed my idea of what it meant to be Italian.

Rome, 1981

AT THE TERMINI STATION in Rome, my brother Bob and I walked over a mile in the dense July heat to a *pensione* called the Adria, recommended to us by neighbors back home. I had just graduated from college, and my brother had offered me the gift of a trip to Europe, an attractive proposal for a New Jersey girl determined to wander farther from home than Steubenville, Ohio, the longest distance we had traveled as a family to celebrate the elaborate weddings of my cousins.

Rome was the final leg of a journey that had begun in England and meandered to Amsterdam, France, and northern Italy. London was the only place I had really wanted to visit, and I displayed the naïve and irritating intellectual snobbery of a twenty-two-year-old, insisting that we find a bed-and-breakfast in Bloomsbury so I could walk along the same paths as Virginia Woolf.

I entered Italy dispossessed of any image of its landscape. I never took the time to dream about the gentle push of water that guides Venetian life, or the rows of olive groves and honey-colored Tuscan fields that elegantly surrender to vast mountain ranges. In my small provincial world, Italy meant fried dough and little ladies dressed in black. My lack of curiosity was in part a reaction to American stereotypes of Italians and perhaps grew out of a subconscious knowledge, based on how my relatives looked and acted, that the home of my grandparents bore little relationship to the land in which I now found myself.

The Adria was located near the station, on the Via Settembre XX, a good distance from most of the city's major attractions, but it was cheap, about twenty dollars a night. The *pensione* was small and dumpy; even taking a shower was an elaborate endeavor. The one shower on each floor had no water handles because the owner of the residence, in an attempt to save money, had removed this essential piece of plumbing. We had to go to the front desk each morning to ask for the handle to turn on the water, and the *padrone*, Papa Adria, as we secretly called him, was visibly annoyed that we made this request daily. One young boy acted as the bellhop, the concierge, the morning deliverer of muddy coffee and crusty rolls, and the person who attached the metal handle to the shower. The *pensione* had business cards that were meant to attract English-speaking tourists, and included a two-word description of the establishment that read: "Nice Place."

Rome's beauty is of the earth, rich in ochers and terra-cottas. It is not classically handsome, and in retrospect, having to fight for a shower handle seems appropriate to my early state of mind; I entered the country a straitlaced promoter of pristine English parks. Confused by the unkept bushes and the absence of perfect rows of flowers throughout the grounds of the Villa Borghese, I was unready for its just-woken-up look, which keeps the ancient beauty young. It took me a while to appreciate the glaucous hue of the Tiber, so unlike its translucent sister, the Seine, but still lovely to walk along, especially in the fall, when the leaves of surrounding trees match the river's color. To be fussy in Rome is a pity; those who are miss its unmatched charm.

After just a day, I allowed myself to open up to Rome, that iridescent, loving, dirty, elegant, tattered, generous city; and I truly felt at home. Along Rome's dusty cobbled streets that left traces of grainy dirt on the soles of sandaled feet, during walks that felt like a stroll on an urban beach, with ruins replacing the immortal properties of water—slow, loving walks—joy replaced doubt and the possibility emerged of a return to the place I had never been: the birthplace of my grandparents.

Many children or grandchildren of immigrants have similar tales to tell, describing that moment of cultural epiphany, the reaffirmation of their link to the past. I may have been at home in Rome simply because I love large cities, and the familiar foods and people gave me a special kind of comfort; I was offered a cozy living room that's never been redecorated, which I could find nowhere else. *Roma puttana*, she is called, Rome the whore, who welcomes all.

"In Rome to go out is to go home," wrote Eleanor Clark in *Rome and a Villa*. Or in the words of a coworker of my brother's from Newark ("Nork"), New Jersey, whom we happened to meet in the light of the Piazza Navona's Bernini fountain as the water gently bubbled and sprayed along its stone basin, "Rome is one big hangout party, just like Bloomfield Avenue in Nork." I discovered that there's no less intimidating way to learn about Italy's high culture than through the open embrace of Rome.

After that trip, Rome became addictive. I needed to travel there and to other parts of northern Italy each year to fortify myself with a taste of the sybaritic café life, to watch dark-haired people dressed with stylish ease, and to hear a language that I had become determined to speak. I became good friends with a couple who lived in the Roman quarter of Trastevere, and I found a residential apartment near them which I would return to for several weeks each summer.

Shopping daily for produce at the outdoor market in the Campo dei Fiori, sitting for hours drinking espresso in the Piazza di Santa Maria in Trastevere, watching life in this open-air museum graced with palm trees and Renaissance art, I repeatedly asked myself the obvious question: How could I have been embarrassed about my heritage if these were my roots? In the United States, Italy almost overnight had become synonymous with food, fashion, and furniture. Finally I had awoken to the beauty of my homeland. I could cling to the memory of Romans strolling by softly lit fountains during their evening *passeggiata* to erase the American image of the guido cruising through the night. Only later would I learn that the blood brother of the guido is the *terrone*, the disparaging name for southern Italian peasants.

Rome, late 1980s

FOR THOSE FEW WEEKS each summer, I claimed as my own the narrow curved roads of Trastevere, once a working-class area that was attracting artists, filmmakers, and journalists with the skill or money to renovate the neighborhood's ancient apartment buildings. This new breed of Trasteverini, intrigued by the quarter's urban grit, lived side by side with the young "Romanacci," bad Romans, who lingered aimlessly by sun-baked fountains, their lithe bodies and angry boy-man faces befitting a Pasolini script. "Arnardo [is] now the very image of Trastevere," wrote Pasolini in his book *Roman Nights.* "Is there anything that can still make his soul—black like his hair—tremble?" In truth, the Romanacci of the eighties were accepted because they were harmless, concerned more with strutting the square in jeans and black vinyl than with encountering the passersby.

In the daytime I would sit at a café in the main piazza and talk to the regulars, would-be filmmakers in beige linen waiting endlessly for the next project, their routine interrupted by the occasional visit to the film studio Cinecittà on the outskirts of Rome, where they went to mingle and find production work. I met people who pointed out to me the hidden contradictions of this secularly spiritual quarter, such as the most recent incarnation of the parsonage attached to the Romanesque church of Santa Maria, thought by some to be the oldest church in the city. The parsonage, which once housed caretakers and served as offices for the clergy, had been rented out as a lingerie showroom for Gianni Versace. Boxes of richly colored satin bikinis, bras, and underwear were carelessly sprawled in these once solemn rooms, and a handsome Milanese sales rep mischievously dangled the skimpiest of the stock, teasing, "Who's going to model this?" At the beginning of the month, a man from the Vatican came by to collect the rent.

At night I had dinner with my friends Daniela and Arie at a little trattoria that served only locals, the owner routinely turning away tourists who happened to stumble upon it. Daniela, a large-framed woman with golden brown hair pulled tightly into a ponytail that glistened in the Roman sun, was fifteen years older than I, childless, and a mother figure to me. A television documentary journalist, Daniela had come to New York in the early eighties with a psychologist colleague (the one who said "sheeps" for ships) to research the conditions of American mental institutions; her trip had coincidentally taken place the week I had written a cover story for my newspaper on the same subject. We met for lunch at a smoky Greenwich Village bar better known for cooking up jazz than for food, and when we said good-bye, Daniela, who was struck by my young age of twenty-three, placed her thick fingers on top of my mine and enveloped me in a firm grip. She invited me to stay with her in Rome, and mesmerized by her consuming presence and generosity, I accepted the offer.

Every year afterward, I saw Rome through Daniela's eyes, for Rome was her city like no other could be.

Daniela guided me through the curves of Trastevere, and like a good Roman, her fervent sense of place meant that, after returning from work at the RAI television station, she would travel no further than her immediate neighborhood, with the occasional exception of a ten-minute stroll to the Piazza Navona (the trip to New York was an aberration). Each night she would carefully negotiate our dinner menu with the owner of the restaurant and then turn to me to continue a lengthy discussion about Italian politics or quote a favorite writer, like G. G. Belli, the nineteenth-century poet, beloved by the people of Trastevere, who had dedicated his work to their neighborhood. Daniela saw it as her job to defend the importance of his playful sonnets, written in Romanesco, the language of Trastevere, against those who dismissed his poetry as trivial and uncouth; her Dutch companion Arie, fluent in English, translated the Italian that I couldn't understand.

"*Allora. Ma io non sono una vera romana* [Ah, but I am not a true Roman]," Daniela would mockingly say after exhibiting an intricate knowledge of the city, emphatically shaking her index finger and slightly trilling her *r*'s with an experienced tongue (Daniela spoke only Italian and French; she tried learning English but thought it an ugly language). True Roman families must have resided in the city for seven generations; Daniela's had lived there for only five. Walking through Trastevere in wide-strap leather sandals, an earth-colored tunic, and clunky African jewelry she had bought at the Porta Portese flea market, Daniela, who always held a lit Marlboro between tobacco-stained fingers, embodied the Roman ideal for me. She was an intellectual free spirit who made every dinner a banquet, overflowing with food, wine, and ideas. In Daniela's presence, no one else mattered; she was the entire show, and in public she never tired or signaled a hint of depression. Sometimes we would drive in Daniela's old gray Deux Chevaux to her family's summer place, a condominium converted from a medieval castle in a small ocean town called Folonica; Daniela was a classic Italian Communist who believed that every worker deserved a country home in Tuscany.

Despite my ease in Rome and my good fortune in finding generous friends, I still felt the need to reinforce my newfound identity, ensuring a permanent place for myself in Italy's culture. I began to daydream about meeting an Italian mate, and entered that phase in my late twenties when, tired of American men, I declared that I would only date someone whose first name ended in o. I proceeded like a racehorse with blinders, straight on, ready to run headfirst into a brick wall of my own making. I had already met Augusto and Giancarlo, foreigners spending part of their time in the United States. Next was Fabrizio, fresh out of school and working for Giancarlo.

Fabrizio was my last, most serious o attachment, who eventually, after far too many shed tears, introduced me to the phenomenon of Italian young men known as *mammoni*, or mama's boys. Usually in their late twenties or thirties, *mammoni* live at home with their mothers until they find her replacement in a woman who, for convenience' sake, is called a wife. Typical *mammoni* from the most urbane places in Italy will tell you, as one told me, that they are unfamiliar with the restaurants in their cities because no one can prepare a better meal than mama does at home. *Mammoni* are not an anomaly but a way of life: the *New York Times* reported on this stay-in-the-nest syndrome, citing a statistic that 50 percent of Italy's twenty-nine-year-olds still live at home.

I met my *mammono* at a party in Rome one October. The evening ended with Giancarlo and Fabrizio stumbling over each other to point out historical treasures during a midnight stroll, and I tried to muster an Audrey Hepburn-like air, walking through streets draped in a veil of soft peach light near the Castel Sant'Angelo. Fabrizio spent the rest of my trip suggesting that he was the man for me, and I agreed, despite our difficulty in communicating because neither of us was fluent in the same language. It did not dawn on me until many months later that I had lost a terribly important tool in understanding who he was: I couldn't make the instant assessments that one normally makes when sizing up a new acquaintance, guessing his background and politics from passing comments and his way of speaking.

Under the dim light of an old chandelier that hung in my rented apartment, I gave a small dinner party to introduce Fabrizio to my Italian friends. I was surprised at how poorly it went, and the less-than-subtle remarks that were made about him afterward. He is very good-looking, they politely said, but the Roman district where his parents lived, the Pratti, is filled with Fascists. Oblivious to his character and wanting to believe that Italians were not foreigners but my people, I ignored the skeptical faces and merrily boiled water for spaghetti. Later that night, when we went out for gelato and *caffè*, the tension between Fabrizio and my friends was palpable. But because I could only understand the broad outlines of conversations in Italian—giant cartoon bubbles, not textured meanings—I thought their antipathy might be based in part on jealousy.

In Italy and back in New York, I was a blissful idiot, already missing the many warning signs Fabrizio gave that trouble lay ahead:

I should have known better when for Christmas he sent me a poster-size collage of pictures—of himself.

I should have known when he wooed me in the Piazza Navona with the line *"Questa piazza è bella perche ci sei tu* [This square is beautiful because you are here]."

I should have known when he decorated his room in his parents' apartment with giant posters of Sylvester Stallone, whom Fabrizio believed he resembled.

I should have known when he brought me half a box of chocolates—the other half having been handed over to his mother.

I should have known better, but at the time I didn't.

When he came to visit me in New York that January, the romance began to wilt, although I still was too infatuated with the idea of Fabrizio to understand that I was craving something that I had spent my life disparaging. I couldn't, for example, make Fabrizio a decent plate of eggs. They would be too runny. He'd shout. I'd try again. They would be too dry. He'd shout. I'd dump the oil and try again. He would tell me to stop trying, and gloomily eat what sat before him.

I couldn't make him an English muffin. Although he had never tasted one, he decided that the bread shouldn't be toasted. I explained that English muffins are only partially baked and need to be toasted. He'd roll his eyes with a look of "These women can't do anything right," so I gave him a raw English muffin. He took a bite of mine with its tiny streams of melted butter running through crunchy golden brown crevices, and stared at the flaccid pale piece of bread in front of him. But refusing to admit defeat, Fabrizio ate his.

Oh yes, and I didn't cook pasta correctly, which he had to have for lunch. It was poorly stirred, a few strands stuck to the pot. If he had stirred the damned spaghetti, I thought, while I was busy preparing something else, we could have avoided this problem, presented as gravely as the matter of the Italian trains not running on time. But I put up with him and his proclivity to flirt with every American woman he met (when I came to greet him at Kennedy Airport, I found Brooke Shields helping him with his passport) because, I must admit, I liked walking hand in hand through the streets of New York with my handsome Roman, my contemporary connection to the mother country.

The silly youthful romance with Fabrizio ended the next summer in Rome, when he abruptly canceled a road trip we were supposed to make throughout Italy ("I must show you properly my country"), informing me that he was interested in the daughter of the ambassador to Kenya ("Do you think it will be a problem for me to date a black woman?"). Fuming, I had to spend an afternoon with him and his friends and listen to their fascinating mealtime discussions: in one conversation they spoke of how Fabrizio's feet shared the odoriferous scent of Gorgonzola cheese if he didn't bathe daily. That night, when I stepped into his car and he yelled at me for tracking dirt from the street onto its floor, I decided that after he drove me to my apartment I would never to speak to him again; and I never did. Not knowing what to do in the days before my departure, I chose melodrama, taking a long bus ride to the outskirts of Rome to visit Hadrian's Villa. There, amid a field of ruins, I found a quiet bench away from the tourists where I sobbed, surrounded by a group of clucking ducks seemingly unmoved by the melancholy of the grounds.

When I think back on the brief era of Fabrizio, it sounds cartoonish; maybe it was. The egocentric man Fabrizio had become seemed less a real person than an amalgam of images he had collected over the course of his young life: the angry husband demanding decent food on the table/the Italian lover with his transcontinental string of women, hindered only by sharing the same roof with mom/the American ideal of the Italian hunk influenced by the Italian-American Sylvester Stallone.

Several years later, during a vacation in Rome, I was getting dressed for dinner, tuning into the usual dreadful lineup of Italian television, when I stumbled upon a popular show called "Numero Uno." The weekly program puts contestants through a series of tests before crowning the winner "number one" in a certain field, and that evening the title being sought was *numero uno casalingua*, number one housewife. The three women who wished to receive this honor had to perform a host of household duties, culminating in a competition at the ironing board. A laundry bag sat before the women, who raced to iron out rumpled cotton for three gorgeous Italian men standing onstage wearing only boxer shorts. I couldn't imagine this starch meet on prime-time American television, and I was reminded again of the stark schism in gender roles in Italy. Pop culture tells young men like Fabrizio to dump a bag of wrinkled laundry in front of a woman and pose while she races to iron it. A prisoner of the image of the Italian man who punches the air declaring "I will make the decisions in this household," Fabrizio had inherited a view of women as old as Latin, in a time in which the words "Ave Maria" meant more than "Hail Mary" ("Ave" backwards is Latin for Eve). Medieval theologians interpreted this conflation of Eve and Mary as a symbol of women's dual role as temptress and Madonna. Fabrizio's narrow expectations similarly excluded any other possibility for women.

In a country where many children still go to school six half-days a week, in part to end the day by one-thirty to ensure a leisurely lunch with mama, I should have understood the odds I was up against in my search for a suitable partner. Overcome by a passion for, and the glamour of Rome, I sought *un' italiano d'Italia*, an Italian from Italy, not an Italian-American, fooling myself into thinking that I shared Fabrizio's heritage, that an Italian partner could erase the hyphen and make me whole. Perhaps I could have assessed this relationship much sooner if I had listened more closely to stories about my southern Italian relatives. A cousin from New Jersey who lived for several years in southern Italy described the familiar scene along the dirt roads of the village where he stayed: the men proudly sat atop donkeys to make their miles-long journey, while the women followed behind, holding the tail of the ass.

Milan, 1995

AT A DINNER PARTY in the Milanese apartment of Paolo and Alessandra, a professor of government and business management at Università Luigi Bocconi and a doctoral candidate there, I am telling a Pat Cooper joke. I laugh to myself at the ludicrousness of repeating the lounge-club humor of this 1960s Italian-American comic. I'm at this dinner party because my husband, who indulges my desire to visit Italy yearly, received an invitation to lecture at the school where Paolo teaches. We are spending a week in northern Italy before heading to Rome.

The gist of the joke is that over the years a young man describes his assortment of girlfriends to his Italian grandmother, although he is doubtful of receiving the old lady's approval. The first girlfriend is Protestant, the second Jewish, the third black. Each time he tells her about these women, she says, "Fine, fine, whatever makes you happy." One day he declares that he's found the perfect bride, and that finally his grandmother will be proud because she is Italian. "Oh really," the grandmother replies gravely, "and what part of Italy is she from?"

Paolo confessed that his father, whose family has lived for generations in the northernmost region of Friuli that borders Austria, was extremely upset when he discovered his son's future wife was a southerner. To Italians, the Pat Cooper joke implies that any woman whose family lives south of Rome is of peasant stock. That's the gentle version of their class distinctions; the harsher attitude is that the inferior *terroni* should go back to the south.

Terrone. The word sounds so benign, literally meaning "of the land," a nurturing connection to the earth that belies the anger of those who use it. *Terrone* is the Italian T-word, as we Americans are accustomed to using an initial to interject a sense of propriety in discussions of prejudice.

Northern Italians have their own jokes about the *terrone.* The writer Tim Parks, an Englishman who lives near Verona and is married to an Italian, described in *An Italian Education* the anger against the southerner that begins at a very young age. His daughter, accustomed to graffiti like *Ruggisce il leone / Trema il terrone* (The northern lion roars / The southern peasant trembles), repeated to him and several neighbors a joke she learned about an American, Scotsman, Italian, and *terrone* in a train compartment (the Italian is the northerner, the *terrone* the southerner). The American pulls out a cigar, takes a few puffs, and tosses it out the window. When asked why he tossed the cigar, he replies, "Oh, we've got so many cigars in America." The Scotsman pulls out a bottle of whiskey, takes a sip, and also tosses it. When asked why he threw the bottle out, he replies, "Oh, we've got so much whiskey in Scotland." The Italian picks up the *terrone* and tosses him out the window. "Why did you do that? He didn't do anything," a train passenger says. In a predictable ending, the Italian replies, "Oh, we've got so many, many *terroni* in Italy."

Parks, who was dismayed by the racist humor, recalled that everyone laughed, if a bit nervously. The reaction sounded similar to the one I caused by telling the Pat Cooper joke at the dinner table. Alessandra had looked wounded. An accomplished twenty-nine-year-old, Alessandra admitted that she didn't realize the degree of prejudice against southerners until she moved to Milan and married into an established northern family.

We laughed at the Cooper joke when I was growing up because Italian-Americans had their own prejudices. Even people who come from the bottom of the abyss keep hoping that there is a place deeper and dimmer than their own pit. My mother's family, from the region of Campania, called themselves Neapolitan; my father's side was from further south, Basilicata, Italy's poorest region. But still, both places were north of Calabria, and everyone knew that the darkest Italians were Sicilian.

Paolo was amused that I could relate to this joke, that I even considered myself Italian. He shares the view of most Europeans that Americans, far too obsessed with their heritage, have little if anything in common with their grandparents or great-grandparents from the nineteenth century. I explained that Americans instinctively identify each other by their ethnic ancestry; we are known as Irish or Italian or German or Puerto Rican, not simply by the bland appellation "American." Italians, on the other hand, have only just begun to tackle this thorny issue of ethnicity and nationality, brought to attention a few years ago when a young black woman who had emigrated from the Dominican Republic was crowned Miss Italy and a judge wanted to rescind her title, arguing that she was not truly Italian.

Another guest at the dinner party asked if I went to Italy every year to visit my relatives in the south.

"No," I replied, "I visit friends in Rome."

I wasn't sure, and would not discover until the following year, that I had relatives living in the south. I didn't want to admit that in nearly fifteen years of coming to Italy, I had made just one disastrous attempt to travel south with my brother during our first trip: we arrived in Naples, and I was so overcome by its chaos and poverty that I insisted we take the next train back to Rome. The earliest train left from another station, and my entire Neapolitan experience consisted of the walk between these two points of entry; I passed enough tenements and beggars to conclude that there was no need to stay even an hour longer.

YEARS AGO I COUNTERED my nearsightedness with an unusual reflex. Confronted with a blurry sign in the distance, instead of peering ahead to see more clearly, I opened my eyes very, very wide. Somehow, the normal inclination to squint to sharpen sight simply eluded me, until a college friend pointed out that I was the only person he knew who went through life with this wide-eyed but failed approach to clear vision.

I think about this old habit of mine when I reflect on the time I spent in Italy in the eighties: how with wide-open eyes I failed to see what lay before me. Convinced that I was "Italian," believing that Rome held a promise for my future because of blood ties from my past, I adopted the image maker's technique of constructing reality from my own myopic view.

Regional animosities have escalated to such a degree in the nineties that the Italian central government adopted changes like creating a new license plate to read "Italia," instead of the generations-old practice of inscribing the name of the city where the owner purchased the car (only a fraction of the cars carry these plates because the interminably slow Italian bureaucracy has had difficulty implementing the plan). One filmmaker depicted his nightmare scenario of Italian classism in a short about a poor northern family and a nouveau riche southern one living in Milan whose differences erupt into a full-scale battle. During what became an armed ethnic clash between the Milanese and the *terroni*, their television sets blared with news reports of the fighting in Bosnia.

I once justified my refusal to travel south by congratulating myself that I had "become" an Italian-American, that it was good enough to no longer be ashamed of the country of my ancestors. Rome was the perfect midpoint between the two disparate worlds of northern and southern Italy, and I performed a kind of cultural eugenics, modifying and enhancing the characteristics of my Italian past. Like the young girl who didn't want to be known as an Italian-American, once again I was an impostor, a cultural thief, hoarding northern Italy's riches as if they were my own.

During the time I spent in Italy, I tried to fashion a life and identity for my ancestors based on how I wanted them to live. I saw hunched old Roman women dressed in black meeting for a morning cappuccino; they looked just like my maternal grandmother, and I envisioned her living simply, but without hardship. I closed my eyes to a life of poverty that was beyond my imagination, the relentless hours working in the fields, the daily difficulties for young women who walked for miles carrying heavy baskets of food on their heads.

I had embraced the Italy of the north, a world away from my roots, blessed by an abundance of natural beauty and fertile land that made a mockery of the useless southern terrain.

Milan, 1997

ONCE AGAIN MY HUSBAND had been asked to teach at Bocconi for several weeks, and we returned to Milan with our five-month-old baby. I had been looking forward to this trip for many months, nervously preparing to travel with an infant, shipping bottles and diapers ahead of time, acquiring tips from parents about the plane ride. But Milan turned cold on me, the late October temperature dipped to the forties, and I was frustrated trying to navigate the city's child-unfriendly terrain, pushing my stroller for half a mile past my destination and speeding cars before I could find a traffic light to cross the street. Finally I could comprehend the astounding statistic that Italy has the lowest birth rate in the world, 1.2 children per family, the figure being even lower in the north because southerners are having the majority of babies. The Milanese, too busy earning money to think about children, are ill equipped for family life; an inadequate public transportation system has resulted in streams of cars that crowd the streets and were double-parked on sidewalks. I stood with my stroller before sidewalks overflowing with Turin steel, clueless as to how I could get by; Milan made New York City look like a giant playground.

My sensitivity to Italy's class distinctions even transformed the stroller I pushed into a symbol of the gulf between the north and the south (albeit, a small, collapsible, navy-with-white-polka-dots symbol). A year and a half earlier in New York, I had found myself besieged by Milanos—not trendy northerners clothed in Prada and Zegna, but a top-of-the-line Ferrari of strollers called the Milano, made by Peg Perego, the Italian manufacturer *de giorno.*

At the time, I didn't know the difference between a collapsible umbrella stroller and a sturdy English pram, but Peg Perego's Milano, large and plush, caught my eye, so I inquired about the finer points of its design. The store salesman told me that Peg Perego made three carriages that convert to sit-up strollers once the baby can support its head: the high-priced Milano, medium-ranged Roma, and least expensive Amalfi. Milano, Roma, Amalfi? At first I couldn't believe what I was hearing: as the model gets cheaper, it's named after a city located further south on Italy's socially charged map. The finest things in life flow from Milan.

To follow the logic of this company, located in the small town of Arcora just outside Milan, shouldn't the Milano and

Roma have been accompanied by the Napoli? But what American would buy a product called the Napoli, which sounds more like a pizzeria than a fancy vehicle in which to place your precious little one. Better to market a product with the name of the breathtaking Amalfi coast than the neighboring city of Naples, known for its poverty and pickpockets.

My up-front stroller salesman promoted the cheaper Amalfi, explaining that the structure of the three carriages was essentially the same, but that at seventeen pounds the Amalfi is easier on parents than the cumbersome twenty-three-pound Milano. At that point, I had needed no further persuasion. The southerner in me began to seethe; I would buy the compact Amalfi, not the showy Milano.

But after my baby was born, I experienced that pang of remorse parents spend a lifetime battling, the sinking knowledge that every decision we make affecting our child isn't perfect. Suddenly Milanos and Romas appeared everywhere. As I sat on park benches, roamed through Baby Gaps, and ordered food in child-friendly restaurants, I saw mothers pushing the elegant, elongated carriage of the Milano past the shorter, squatter body of my southern Amalfi. Milano babies didn't seem to cry; they just wriggled miniature arms and legs in the roomiest seats.

When we flew to Milano carrying the six-pound-lighter Amalfi, I decided to conduct some informal research on Italian strollers while my husband taught a morning class. I went to a spacious two-story children's shop a few blocks from our residence to examine a floor filled with Italian carriages. No Milanos, Romas, or Amalfis were in sight. A saleswoman, only vaguely familiar with the models, told me that they weren't sold in Italy. As I imagined, and our friend Paolo agreed, Peg Perego could never get away with naming a cheaper line of products "Roma" and

"Amalfi" in Italy. Instead, I was surrounded by the Italian-made version of giant English prams, and learned that Peg Perego's chief competitor is a company called "Inglesina," which means a little English girl.

All parents project a piece of themselves on their offspring, hoping to create a value system in a chaotic, impersonal world through child-rearing choices, so naturally our cultural biases get transferred to the products that we buy. In Milan, I discovered that Peg Perego's carriage/stroller line wasn't available because jittery parents, unlike their American counterparts, consider the product too flimsy to transport newborns and infants: Italian parents want to push giant English prams during their evening *passeggiata.* New Yorkers, on the other hand, typically choose a stylish Italian model over a more familiar American brand—and an Italian manufacturer markets a product for Americans that reflects its own sense of class and entitlement.

Difficult as it was to maneuver my baby around the streets of Milan, I was delighted that I had a few less pounds to lug each time I performed the parental circus act of collapsing the stroller while juggling infant and diaper bag to get into a taxi or on a bus. And my little boy, never having experienced the bit of luxury offered by the Milano, gurgled contentedly inside his stroller, which I decided that dreary Milanese October to rename the Napoli.

Throughout this trip, it seemed that everyone we talked to wanted to move; Paolo and Alessandra had a wonderful old apartment close to the university decorated in a sparse white Milanese style. But the rent was very high and they were tired of having to raise their three-year-old daughter in a place that has fewer parks than most other European cities. Alessandra told me that if you are elderly, disabled, or a child, there is little room for you in self-sufficient Milan. A woman who was eight months pregnant complained about the city at a dinner party we attended, re-marking that after her daughter was born they would spend much of their time at her family's Tuscan cottage.

What had happened to me? I wondered. I used to love com-ing to Milan, but now the city felt hard, shallow, ugly in the rain. I imagined Rome, warmer in spirit and climate, but I still couldn't see myself strolling with an infant on its polluted roads packed with tiny cars and noisy Vespas. Even Daniela, my Roman teacher, had moved out of Trastevere, having tired of the crowds and the noise. I hadn't seen her in years; after I married I believe she felt that her role as my protector had been usurped, and she rarely travels to Rome from her new home, fifty minutes away.

After we had settled in, I began to find familiar comforts and became calmer, seeking out Milan's pleasures beneath the city's crusty exterior. Pushing a baby stroller gave me a status that I had desperately sought years before; every day I was stopped on the streets, thought to be a native, and asked for directions. But for this trip Italian words would not emerge from my lips, I could only sputter a *"Non lo so."*

I used to act like a daughter in Italy, not a mother, and the adjustment challenged me daily. The time for transformation had ended. Daughters are insouciant, mothers measured; now my Ital-ian days were guided by the rhythms of another life. The Roman nights of my twenties, nights that were lonelier than their glow in my memory, had faded with the small pang of regret that ac-companies the end of a fantasy. I had longed to be a European— not a southern European, like my ancestors, but the cultivated western ones I had met in Rome. But as a not-so-young mother visiting Milan, preoccupied with nursing my baby, unwilling to shop for my post-pregnant self, the glamour of the city had dis-sipated, as did the need to possess an exotic past. Instead came a new realism: one's origins are not romantic. Like the act of birth, they're merely the seeds of the life we're given—messy, tumultuous, mundane.

At the end of our stay, my husband was offered the opportunity to work in Milan. Years ago I dreamed of living in Italy, and possibly that would have been the time to become an expatriate American who could think she was Italian; or perhaps in our future I might comfortably find a place for myself there as an Italian-American. For the moment, we were flattered, briefly entertained the idea, and knew we had to go home.

Words

Each time I traveled to Italy, I longed to use the correct Italian grammar and speak with just a trace of an accent—a goal far beyond my reach. I learned Italian in my late twenties, by which point my brain was too rusty and my tongue too lazy to form new sounds. I also carried with me an assortment of dialect words from my childhood, and I tried them out on my Italian friends, expecting downturned Roman smiles and knowing nods that signaled camaraderie. My friends, however, were befuddled, unable to decipher what I was saying. Their confused stares confirmed that I had once again committed some gross violation of their language; and the look on their faces brought back my sense of childhood shame about dialect.

Shame seems to me to play an important part in the way many Italian-Americans have come to see themselves in relationship to the larger world. The Italian-American searches for social status and intellectual respectability, hoping to escape a role cast long ago for the dark white ethnic. When I was a child, we tried to mask our susceptibility to shame by keeping "ethnic" details, the keys to our identity, under lock and key. Secrets and shame converged daily in our use of southern Italian dialect.

WE SPOKE ONLY ENGLISH at home, but my parents kept alive an assortment of southern Italian dialect words that signaled a quiet intimacy or set off the alarms of subterfuge. Dialect was our private language, stranger than pig Latin, which at least had its own set of rules; and as with any secret, there were pleasures in knowing and tensions in keeping it. These homegrown foreign words captured the musings and jags of daily life but had to be uttered solely among ourselves.

"Do you understand me? Are you *stunod*?" my mother would say.

Stunod. Someone who is out-of-it, spacey, not a practical person who knows that life is labor and that only the sturdy can get the job done. You lock the keys in the car. You pause, ponder, lose the moment instead of seizing it. You're *stunod.* Because I only heard dialect at home, these words had an unreal quality—did they exist or were they imaginary? There was no dictionary for me to look them up in, so I slowly allowed dialect to form a shape in my mind, an embryo whose meaning eventually became clear. *Stunod.* The playful, secret word danced in my head, twirling, twirling, one step, two steps, pirouette—*thump.* Then I understood the meaning of *stunod,* and what it said about me.

Thump. Dialect stung like a playground tumble, these forceful assertions about human nature left little room for the timid. Various layers of meanings filled the words, making it hard to find an English equivalent as rich as the choice in dialect. You can be momentarily *stunod,* or the word can describe a general state of mind that applies both to the ethereal dreamer and to someone who's a little slow. Or a person, like a nonstop talker, can make you *stunod*, the type who consumes so much of the room's oxygen that you're left gasping for air. To me, the emotional clarity of each meaning is so perfect that I have kept this word in my adult vocabulary, and share it with my Russian Sephardic Jewish American husband who immediately understands my linguistic shorthand when I declare a person *stunod*.

My American-born parents grew up communicating with their parents, whose knowledge of English was extremely limited, in southern Italian dialect (actually, my father listened to his parents' dialect and responded in English). After my grandparents died, my mother and father had little reason to speak what they knew was not the "real" Italian, Tuscan Italian, but the language of an illiterate people from the south of Italy. And it would have been difficult for my parents to speak to each other solely in dialect because there were differences in the languages they had learned growing up. Their parents came from towns only about forty miles apart, but each had a distinct dialect, nurtured for centuries by separate cultural influences and foreign rule. My parents' marriage put this fractured history behind them; their children would speak only in English.

It was impossible, however, for my mother to keep her beloved dialect in storage, and a steady stream of words emerged throughout the day. When I refused to change my mind about something, she called me *gabbadotz*. When tired and unresponsive, I was *mooshamoosh*. If I grabbed too many free samples in the food store, I was acting like a *mortitavahm*. The runny-nosed, scabby-kneed kids who ran around our block were *squistamod*. What a *bijanzee!* she'd say to describe the magnitude of our family problems. Dropping a plate, stubbing her toe, or encountering any stumbling block to getting the housework done, my mother let out a cry of *footitah*. I was left to fill in the blanks, to figure out the general category of emotion to which the word belonged. A word like *gabbadotz* was easy, that meant stubborn, but the others were trickier, eluding a one-word English definition.

Despite the harsh assessments, when my mother used dialect the gesture was affectionate, not a reprimand. I was comforted to hear words spoken only between us, that no one else knew. The tone was often humorous, sometimes ironic, an interpretation of the world which my parents were passing along to their children.

But I also understood that I would face undue embarrassment if our code of silence was broken, if I repeated dialect to outsiders. Suburbanites say hello to passersby and comment on the lovely day; they entertain with barbecues and bring out steaks and corn on the cob; but they don't speak or eat like peasants, and we had to imitate their behavior. I could get myself into trouble if I used odd-sounding words or told neighbors about the strange foods that I devoured.

My love of my mother's cooking (many of the dishes felt doubly foreign because they had dialect names) and her expressive use of southern Italian provided the simmering flavors of a life that I never knew but felt intimately connected to. But at the same time, southern Italian food and dialect words, my closest cultural links to our past, collided with everyday life in our suburban cul-de-sac. And as a child, I realized that I couldn't afford to repeat the kind of mistake that I had made with Joey Unger.

Joey Unger was our neighbor and my brother Bob's junior high school pal, whose family moved to our town, my parents told me, because his father had a very important job as an engineer building the Verrazano Narrows Bridge. During one of Joey's regular visits to our house, I joined him and my brother on the front steps. I was always a bit of an annoyance, being eight years younger than they were, but that afternoon I managed to nudge my way into the conversation.

"What's your favorite food?" Joey asked me.

As I was about to answer, my lips pronouncing the first syllable, I felt a large hand firmly cover my mouth, preventing me from even turning my head. I could barely breathe, let alone respond to Joey. Momentarily confused and afraid, I soon realized that the arm connected to the smothering hand on my mouth was Bob's. How could my kind and affectionate brother be trying to suffocate me? Was I going to die right there on our front stoop while attempting, desperately, earnestly attempting, to tell Joey Unger that my favorite food in the entire world was chicken feet? With my brother's hand rudely clamped on my face, it was impossible to explain how I loved to suck on the wrinkly claws shriveled as a witch's finger steeped in tomato sauce, and describe my favorite part, the large chewy piece of cartilage at the base of the foot, which slid around my teeth with each satisfying bite. It never occurred to me that others might not have tasted this food, a dish common among southern Italian farmers like my grandparents, who raised their own game before settling in New Jersey.

My muffled screams became louder and louder: "Chicken feet. Chick-ken feeet. CHICKEN FEEEET."

"Chicken?" Joey asked.

"Yes, that's right," my brother said. "She loves chicken."

"No, no," I said, shaking my head forcefully, my long hair slapping my face. Chicken couldn't be my favorite food; it was dry and tasteless compared to the lower reaches of the bird.

"Chicken FEEEEEET."

"Chicken something," said Joey, a bit confused.

"Chicken FEEEEEEEEEEET."

"Did she say chicken feet?"

"No, she didn't," my brother responded, his hand still wrapped around my telltale mouth.

I began to violently nod yes.

"She eats chicken feet?" Joey said, scrunching up his boyish white face as if he had never heard anything quite so disgusting.

"I don't know what she's talking about," my beet red brother replied as he opened the screen, deposited me inside the house, and slammed the door. I ran up the steps furious about my mistreatment and watched them walk down the street, my teary face plastered against the windowpane.

OUR ANCESTORS WERE PEOPLE who worked the land, and even if my father had been born in Millburn, New Jersey, even if he had never touched the hilly terrain of Picerno in southern Italy that yielded barely enough crops for them to eat, somewhere deep in his blood was the instinct to pick edible food wherever it was available. As a boy, my father worked weekends as a caddy at a fancy golf club that restricted Italian-Americans and other swarthy types. An enterprising twelve-year-old, one day he discovered a fertile patch of green off the silky eighteen-hole course. He quietly sat on this less traveled path and began to pull up *chicoy*, our dialect word for dandelions that are eaten as a salad.

"What are you doing?" asked one of the golfers who happened to walk by.

"I'm picking these for tonight's dinner," he said.

"You eat grass?" the incredulous golfer replied.

Yes, my father nodded, too embarrassed to explain the satisfying bitter taste of *chicoy* or lie when caught green-handed.

The shame that my father must have felt on that golf course as a child was, in a diluted form, passed along to me, contained in the nervous grip of my brother's hand on my mouth. My father munched on weeds, I ate the feet of chickens; neither was appropriate in our town, either in the roaring twenties or the rebellious sixties. My brother recalls that my mother never cooked chicken feet again after the Joey Unger incident; my parents were mortified to have been caught serving such a low-rent meal. Their shame turned everyday acts into small secrets, as we lived out the stereotype of trusting only the family: don't mention our foods; don't use our dialect words.

This decision caused some emotional trepidation because I would find myself refraining from mentioning subjects as innocuous as a dinner meal. How could I tell friends that my dinner had been a dish made with *kookazeel*? The word sounded more like baby talk than baby zucchini (*cucuzzielli* in dialect, I discovered years later), which my mother sautéed with peppers, onions, and eggs, calling the mixture *jombought*. I had to devise my own rules of nomenclature: if asked about last night's supper, I would describe in general terms what I had eaten, but I'd never assign a name to the dish.

Lettuces seemed bound to get my family in trouble in America. In high school I became friends with an Italian-American girl whose parents lived on the right side of the tracks but still indulged in, I discovered, the foods of the wrong side.

"Do you eat beans and greens?" she asked me one day.

"What's beans and greens?" I replied.

"Oh, it's a soup my mother makes with escarole and beans."

Meneste, I thought to myself. I've finally met someone else who eats *meneste*.

I loved *meneste*. My mother made it every Monday night, this thick soup of escarole, *cannellini* beans soaked in olive oil, and sliced pepperoni which we sopped up with chunks of soft Italian bread. It was considered a poor person's soup because the ingredients were so cheap (although a less tasty version of this dish sells for $4.50 a pint in Balducci's today). *Meneste*, from the dialect word *menesta*, which means vegetables boiled for soup, looked quite unattractive, with lumps of mushy white beans separating from their filmy skin and seaweed-colored escarole floating in the plate. To me, *meneste* was a delicious mess. I loved the dish, but would never mention it to anyone else.

Beans and greens, however, sounded American, fine to say.

"Yes, my mom makes that too!" I replied with childlike enthusiasm, delighted by a connection that made my household seem less foreign.

"What do you call it?" she asked curiously.

I'm not sure if my friend was testing me, trying to find out if my family, like hers, had an arsenal of embarrassing, hushed-up words. Was "beans and greens" a code phrase, a rhyming sobriquet that could unite us in a shared ancestry and common dialect? Or was her family more "modern" than mine, knowing the dish only by this name?

"Oh, we don't call it anything," I replied, playing it safe.

I'd soon rename the dish "beans and greens," which, unlike *meneste*, was much less of a mess to explain.

DEEPLY UNCERTAIN ABOUT MY place in the world, I couldn't make the self-confident leap in early adulthood to have fun with dialect, to give others a taste of my culture through its language. In my job as a newspaper reporter, the only woman among a group of scruffy men, I once offered a colleague one of my mother's homemade *tatalles. Tatalles* is an Italian-American word for the southern Italian food known as *taralli,* which are made with flour, eggs, olive oil, fennel seed, and pepper. Pieces of this thinly rolled dough are shaped into circles, boiled, and then baked until a crispy golden brown.

I handed a *tatalle* to a newspaper man who spent his day editing words, and he asked the obvious question: "Thanks. And what is this called?"

"It's an Italian pretzel," I responded.

"I've never seen this. What's its name?"

"I don't know," I fumbled, never a good liar.

"It must have a name."

"It's an Italian version of a bagel."

"How can you not know what it's called?" he repeated, exasperated by my food comparisons.

"I don't know its name," I replied, and walked away.

Unwilling to yield this private piece of myself, I couldn't answer this man whose persistence irritated me. I was afraid of being laughed at if I said *tatalle*, an odd-sounding word spoken only at the kitchen table. By keeping dialect separate from my daily discourse, I both increased its importance, allowing me to hold secrets that no one else possessed, and devalued its relevance, believing that I would be taken less seriously if I repeated illegitimate words.

Traveling to Italy helped me relax enough to discuss dialect with an Italian-American college friend, third-generation like myself, who was then a medical school resident. I often teased him because he identified himself as "English and Italian," with the stress on the former (he's about a quarter English); and it was a sign of our close friendship that he felt comfortable enough to share a few of his secret words.

"I remember as a child playing 'Follow the big *gedrool*,'" he said. My friend described how he and close family friends, whom he called cousins, tagged behind his "uncle," the big *gedrool*, a role that might be compared to the part Steve Martin played in *The Jerk*. I immediately laughed, as I do anytime I hear these private words used outside my parents' house. Neither of us had any sense of the history of this language, which began to feel more and more like play money, a fake currency, tossed around only for fun. Was it a kind of Italian-American Yiddish, a mixture of dialects borrowed from several sources, that is part of our vernacular, the *shtetl* meeting the *paese*? But Yiddish, a medieval language once spoken by vast numbers of people from nations as diverse as Germany and Russia, became a common denominator of Jewish culture, is taught in universities, and claims its own literature. Because so few Italian-Americans openly use dialect, I could only confirm its existence by listening to my family or when randomly encountering a person who retains these words in everyday discourse. (Today I can tune in to dialect watching "The Sopranos.") A man at a pay phone says excitedly, "Okay, okay, I'll call the *mamaluke*." *Mamaluke*. Or is it spelled *mamaluch*? Or is spelling irrelevant in an oral language? I wonder how many other New Yorkers have encountered a *mamaluke*, someone, that is, who's a bit soft in the head. It wasn't until I traveled to the south of Italy and met a scholar in Naples whose father, like my maternal grandparents, grew up in a village near Avellino that I discovered the etymology of many of my dialect words.

THE DRAB GRAY FACADE of Università Federico II looks like many old Neapolitan buildings, its color indistinguishable from the endless stream of smoke that spills each day from car exhausts. Inscribed on the entrance archway are the words "Faculty of Letters and Philosophy," yet I initially missed the venerable introduction, focusing instead on the scrawl of graffiti that filled the lower half of the walls. Through the arch was an emerald-green courtyard, and students breathed in this small offering of peace, their heads bowed over books. I made my way past them, turning into a corridor of staircases and walking up three stories of old cement to the philology department. In one of the small cramped offices shared by several faculty members, Professor Nicola De Blasi was waiting for me.

This gentle man, who looked to be in his early forties and was dressed in a professorial dark blue blazer, sweater vest, and wool trousers, would unlock the origins of my secret words. A philologist trained in the love of learning, De Blasi was naturally frustrated that he couldn't speak English well enough to converse with me about the history of Italian dialects. This left us to my Italian, no better than what a university course and several language houses can offer. We hesitantly forged ahead, trying to understand one another, and for the most part succeeded in our discussion of the dialects of Italy.

Italy was divided for many centuries by the accents and speech patterns of regional Latin dialects. It seems only appropriate that Dante, writing in a language of transcendence, would be the man who converted all of Italy to the Tuscan tongue. While Florence during the time of Dante was a growing commercial center, scholars have argued that it was his genius more than the special characteristics of the city that solidified Tuscany's linguistic dominance. As Ernst Pulgram noted in his book *The Tongues of Italy*, "If Dante had been a child of Naples, and providentially, Boccaccio and Petrarch also, Neapolitan and not Tuscan would have become Italy's national language."

In the late nineteenth and early twentieth century, when my grandparents left Italy, they would have spoken, like the vast majority of immigrants, the southern dialects of their regions; and my grandparents knew that their language was thought of in America and in their homeland as substandard Italian. Even in the eighties, when Ciriaco De Mita, who also grew up in the province of Avellino, served as Italy's prime minister, my Roman friends routinely scoffed at his accent and traces of dialect, shaking their heads at the difficulty of understanding the nation's leader. According to De Blasi, the differences in De Mita's pronunciation were small. The former prime minister might have changed a single letter in certain words: for example, in his native dialect, *montagna*, or mountain, would become *mondagna*. De Blasi, however, is a southerner sensitive to the notion that one regional dialect is somehow "better" than another. While emphasizing that all dialects today are less important than the standard Italian, he explained that centuries ago, when dialects flourished, each had a literary as well as a popular form. But that doesn't stop northerners and southerners from making judgments about the worth of each other's words.

The words that I learned growing up were not pure southern Italian dialect (*mamaluke*, for example, is *mammalucco* in dialect). Their roots are in my grandparents' language, but the pronunciations changed over time, as an American tongue prevailed, abandoning old-world sounds for the strange hybrid of Italo-American speech. Like a hothouse lily, this Italian-American lingua franca was bred from the regional dialects of southern Italy, gradually mixing with the vowel off-glides and staccato rhythms of English speech. The information shouldn't have surprised me; but when you grow up hearing dialect, you assume, or at least I did, that the language was Italian, spoken somewhere in Italy. All the pieces of my life considered to be "Italian"—the food, the dialect, the dark hair—I kept distinct from the American side, forgetting about the hyphen, about that in-between place where a new culture takes form.

I had typed a list of dialect words for the professor, and I cautiously began with my favorite.

Stunade, I wrote, a bad transcription because the sound is closer to *stunod*.

He stared at the word, looking quizzical.

Stew-nod, I pronounced carefully, allowing him to examine what my American tongue had done to his dialect.

"*Si, Si, Si*," he responded. "*Stonato. Fuori da testa.*"

"Yes!" I restrained myself from pounding the desk in my enthusiasm. I had found a wizard who made my words real.

Out of one's mind. In dialect, *stonato* means a person who can't understand anything because he is senile or doddering, and is used to describe anyone who acts a little out of it. In Tuscan or standard Italian, the professor explained, the word *stonato* exists, but its meaning changes. *Stonato* is a person who sings off-key, the opposite of *intonato*.

As the intimacies of language bridged the gap between native and foreigner, professor and student, De Blasi became my linguistic confidant. I handed him my list of household dialect words and he began to decipher my connections to the south of Italy. I stated each word, and he repeated it, sometimes several times, listening to the sound, shifting the stress until he was able to recognize its source in the original dialect of my grandparents.

I learned that one reason why my northern friends didn't understand my southern dialect is that many of these words, which all have Latin roots, exist in standard Italian but without the pejorative connotations found in the south. Mentioning a word like *stunod* to my Roman friends, I was asking them to find the link between a person who is mentally confused and one who sings badly. The same problem exists with *citrulo* (pronounced "cheetrool-oh"), southern dialect for the standard Italian *cetriolo*, cucumber. In the north, the word has no metaphorical meaning, but in the south, where it's impossible to separate the people from the land they cultivate, *citrulo* describes a person whose brain is as fleshy and watery as a cucumber.

The Italian-American version of this southern word, in which the *ci* sound changes to a soft *g*, is *gedrool* (as in my friend's childhood game "Follow the big *gedrool*," or "Follow the big cucumber head"). Anyone who has ever listened to that 1950s Anglo-Saxon paean to Italian-American culture, "Mambo Italiano," which continually creeps into contemporary movie sound tracks, would have encountered the *gedrool*. As Rosemary Clooney swooned in her fake Italian-American accent: "Hey *gedrool*, you donnuh have to go to school. / Just make it with a big bambino. It's like a vino / Kid you're good-ah lookin. But you donnuh know what's cookin."

Other vegetable words, like deep purple eggplant, in dialect *mulignan'*, describes black people; and fennel, *finucch* in dialect, is used for gays. I often heard *gedrool* growing up, but I was unaware of the figurative meaning of these other two words. My brother Bob, who is an assistant prosecutor in Newark, New Jersey, tells a favorite office story about the importance of understanding the metaphoric meaning of dialect: An old Italian-American man who spoke broken English went to the police station to file a complaint that he had been attacked by a big *mulignan'*. The officer took down the story verbatim and later asked a colleague, "What is *mulignan'*?" The final report read that the man had been assaulted by a large eggplant.

WITH THE PROFESSOR'S HELP, I was discovering a set of rules that enabled me to link my hand-me-down words to a real language. For example, the standard Italian word *cafone* (cah-fone-ay), meaning an ignorant person, is pronounced "cah-fone" in the south, where the final vowel, always used in standard Italian, trails off. In the Italian-American pronunciation, the hard *c* changes to a hard *g*, and becomes another one of my favorite dialect words, *gavone.*

Understanding this pattern, I discovered why we called the pie my mother made the night before Easter *pizza gain*. I remember how my mother would chide herself all day if she had mistakenly tasted its prosciutto filling on the meatless Good Friday, and how we voraciously ate thick slices of *pizza gain* after returning from Saturday night confession. My dislike of confession compared to my love of this pie could not be measured with worldly cups and tablespoons, but it was worth any penance to commune with this mixture of mozzarella, parmigiano, and ricotta cheese, egg, peppery salami, and prosciutto baked in a crunchy bread shell. The words *pizza gain* made no sense to the American ear, so the dish remained nameless to outsiders, added to the list of family culinary secrets. Fortunately, when I was in high school quiche Lorraine came into fashion, allowing me to serve *pizza gain* to my friends as "a kind of Italian quiche."

In southern dialect, the *pi* (pee) sound in standard Italian often changes to *chi* (key). So the word *piena*, meaning full, becomes *chiena*. *Pizza chiena*, stuffed full of good things, sounds like *pizza gain* to the Italian-American ear. Northern Italians would describe a similar type of pie as *pizza imbottita*.

De Blasi went on translating with blooming vigor, as if he were rediscovering the ties between southern Italians like himself and his transplanted countrymen. I learned that when my mother called me *mooshamoosh*, she was using the dialect *muscia* in its superlative form, *muscia muscia*, meaning a woman who is weak and slow in doing something. (In standard Italian, similar words are *floscia*, meaning soft, and *mogia*, downcast and dejected.) On really lethargic days, I was *mezzamaught*, derived from the dialect *mezzo morta*, or half dead.

Gabbadotz comes from the dialect expression *capa tosta*, literally, having a hard head (*testa dura* in standard Italian). Another frequently used word, *gabbafresch*, which captured my mom's jealousy of carefree women, was probably derived from *capa* (head) and *fresca* (cool or fresh in standard Italian, but which in dialect can mean a woman who chatters aimlessly and works idly).

The reference to snotty-nosed *squistamod* kids is from the dialect *scostumato*, meaning poorly raised and educated. My inclination to act like a *mortitavahm* when gobbling down free food comes from *morto di fame*, literally dying of hunger and used to describe someone disgraced by poverty. And *bijanzee* seems to be derived from *pazienza,* patience, meaning a problem that requires a lot of it.

What about her much repeated *footitah?*

"*Brutta parola,*" said Professor De Blasi, shaking his head.

I tensed watching his expression. Had I just unwittingly handed the professor of philology a curse word?

De Blasi explained that *footitah* is derived from the dialect verb *fottere,* which means "go to the devil." My mother was using the second-person imperative form of the verb. My make-believe words not only had real meaning but were branches of a fiery grammatical tree: *futtiti,* or "you go to hell." Yet I could tell from De Blasi's reaction that *footitah* exerted more force than merely going to hell in a handbasket. I later mentioned *footitah* to Alessandra, our Milanese friend who grew up in the south, and she tittered upon hearing the word. *Futtiti,* she explained, is interpreted as "fuck you" (as opposed to *fanculo,* or go fuck yourself).

Fuck you? My mother only spelled out the F-word: "He said ef-you-see-kay" was the construction we heard throughout our childhood. Yet under the veil of dialect, *footitah* hit the air several times a day.

Dialect must have been a relief, a kind of escape for my mother. After many exhausting years of trying to fit into American culture, she could return to the comfortable language of childhood, when life is as plain as your parents' voice. To be raised by the sturdy hands and ancient customs of people from a primitive culture creates an adulthood of confused aspirations and conflicting values. What a simple luxury, especially in moments of frustration, to slip into one's peasant tongue, allowing language to transport you to the cozy safety of the past.

When I use a dialect word, I am repeating the sounds of my

grandparents—perhaps the closest contact I could have with them. I am now their young grandchild, uttering playful words, oblivious to the meaning of what I am saying. How could I have understood all those years ago, innocently mixing my own batch of sounds, that dialect brought their faraway culture to our little white house, making us, in some tiny way, carriers of their abandoned way of life?

Early each morning, when my father left for work, my mother said he had to "go *zappa*," to put the food on the table. I always sensed that the word had more power than plain work. Decades later, finding a dictionary of the dialect of Picerno, I saw that *zappá* was a dialect form of the standard Italian verb *zappare*, meaning to hoe.

To hoe? My father, like the rest of the commuter dads, took the train to downtown New York to work as a manager of international shipping for the Allied Chemical Corporation. I don't think he knew how to use a hoe. But he had to go *zappa*, literally to labor in the fields, the exacting ritual of rural mountain people. If my mother had said "got to go work in the fields," we would have questioned her grasp of reality. But *zappa* made sense, good sense. My mother's word choice, her interpretation of the meaning of work, unconsciously restored the lost culture of her parents.

Other dialect words are etched permanently into my brain, ensuring that when I react intensely to a situation, with the kind of raw, unfiltered feelings I am embarrassed to possess, dialect, not English, surfaces. If I see a woman who is well taken care of, doesn't work, and wants round-the-clock help to care for her children, clean the house, and cook the meals, I think, "What a *bubidabetz!*" A pampered woman. This is my mother and grandmother and, I'm certain, my great-grandmother talking, and I pinch myself trying to summon up tolerance but can't: I am conditioned to think that a woman who doesn't work hard is a *bubidabetz*. Of course, my ancestors would consider me a *bubidabetz* if they compared my American life to the one they led. I know of no male equivalent of the *bubidabetz*, perhaps because Italian men were supposed to be pampered, and if they weren't, a woman wasn't doing her job properly.

Bubidabetz. Saying the word is fun; it's like blowing bubbles, as I am puffing the aspirated *b*, which sounds like a *p*, sending forth the foamy anger into the air, an ephemeral burst of envy. I'm in a nether region of language, taking words from a nineteenth-century foreign land which have been passed on orally, using them to judge contemporary American culture.

The word *bubidabetz* stumped Professor De Blasi, and he wondered if it might be derived from the name of a character in an Italian folktale. I think, however, I found the origin of *bubidabetz* after meeting my mother's cousins in southern Italy. I also gave them my list of words, and they couldn't stop laughing, surprised at the curious spellings and the thought that remnants of the family's Italian past existed in America.

BOO-bid-ah-betz. I pronounced the word several times.

"Ah," said cousin Franco, listening carefully. *"Pupa di pezza."* A *pupa di pezza* is dialect for a doll with a head and body of stuffed rags and arms made of rags or corn husks. This cheap doll is what poor people give to their children. In a pejorative usage, a woman who is a *pupa di pezza* squanders what has been given to her; she doesn't understand the value of anything.

As I decipher the meanings of my childhood language, I'm bombarded with relentless negativity, notes of jealousy, belittling quips; these are no Hallmark card messages for a warm and fuzzy day. The culture of southern Italy, in which hope was as elusive as fertile land, may have created a special place in language for expressions that let judgment and envy free. De Blasi joked that dialect descriptions are often derogatory because if you thought highly of someone, there was no need to say anything at all.

Not a bad code for exploited, exhausted peasants to live by. Which suggests another interpretation. The words are sharp, funny, distinctly Italian, absent the self-righteous quest for moral perfection found in nineteenth-century American life, and yet filled with a belief in the ultimate worth of human beings. The opposite of the *citrulo* is the self-examining mind. The *pupa di pezza* corrupts industry; the *scostumato* debases communal values; the *morto di fame* maximizes self-pity. Like a diptych, the well-lived life hangs on the opposite hinge, a knowledge so implicit that no words are necessary; honor lives in silence. Isaac Bashevis Singer noted in his eloquent homage to Yiddish that one can find "a gratitude for every day of life, every crumb of success, each encounter of love." The same can be said for the dialects of southern Italy.

DIALECT IS STILL USED in the south but almost everyone knows standard Italian, a linguistic change that gained political force under Mussolini, who wanted the entire country to speak the same language. When I traveled to the town of Conza della Campania in the province of Avellino to meet my maternal cousins, I had hoped to hook them up with my mother by telephone. From the home of her first cousin Concetta Conte, I dialed the States so that she and my mother, Connie Laurino (born Concetta Conti), could talk to each other for the first time in their lives. "Concetta *a* Concetta" I declared, dialing AT&T's "USA Direct" to make sure these two septuagenarians were part of the global connection.

"Try to remember some dialect," I told my mother on the other end. "She doesn't know any English."

My husband pulled out the camera to record the momentous

scene, and I stood next to this tiny woman who barely reached the phone, which sat atop a television set perched on a wooden stand. *"Non capisco, non capisco,"* Concetta repeated. My mother, to no avail, was recalling the dialect from her childhood. Her first cousin, in return, mixed standard Italian and contemporary southern dialect, which was incomprehensible both to me and to my mother. The conversation ended at its inception, and my mother felt saddened—and betrayed, I imagine—that she wasn't understood. My mother said that as soon as she hung up, she telephoned another cousin in New Jersey to repeat the dialect she had used with her cousin in Italy. At least the New Jersey cousin recognized her words as the language of their youth, a partial consolation. My grandparents' archaic nineteenth-century dialect no longer exists in Italy; it, too, is a relic of the past.

Yet the few words—the funny, bitter, expressive words of criticism or emotional release—that I carry with me still resonate in these two distinct cultures. In Conza, when I presented my dialect list to Franco, there was a hush around the kitchen table, and the eyes of the large extended family were all focused on him. After he eliminated the Italo-Americanisms and repeated the words as they pronounce them, my cousins laughed uproariously, recognizing our profound similarities.

I taped his pronunciations and played them for my parents when I returned to the States. At their kitchen table, I watched for a few brief minutes as the distance in time and place disappeared, my mother slapping her knee with enthusiasm, my father's normally unruffled demeanor transformed by laughter. What they heard brought them closer to their parents' lives than any photo I could have shown or story I could have told.

The joy, the unrepressed laughter were the same at both tables; for a moment we sat together, breaking bread, privileged coconspirators sharing a private language, as innocent as children testing the boundaries of appropriate words. To my cousins, our mutual dialect suggested a possibility never before imagined: that the disparate lives of agrarian Italians and suburban Americans were united by similar snap judgments, playful teasing, peasant foods, anger and despair. All were part of both our worlds, expressed by variations of the same words; language filled the gulf between us. To my parents, an identity left behind, a land never seen were given a voice and a place, confirmed by a tiny recorder sitting on Formica that played a piece of their past.

When I attempt to speak the "real" Italian, I stumble to find agreement between subject and verb, throwing pronouns like baseballs, hoping to hit the correct form. I have tried to replace my dialect words with standard Italian, saying *cafone* for *gavone*, *testa dura* for *gabbadotz*, affectionately calling my son Michael *Michele*, not *Miguel*. But I know that my American tongue cannot trill an *r* or shape the lush vowel sounds intended for each syllable, so soon enough I fall back on dialect, those secrets from my youth, that comfortable place between heredity and environment, necessity and chance.

Bensonhurst

> Then said the Great Gamelegs at last . . .
> you offer terms I cannot well refuse.
>
> HOMER, *The Odyssey*

I. RAGE

I keep returning to Bensonhurst, to the narrow wooden and brick row houses that define these working-class streets, but the mental map I create vanishes as soon as I leave. Then Bensonhurst draws me back, a clean slate, ready to fill me again with the marks of a culture that I have previously erased. I wonder what role chance plays in creating an ethnic identity. Does growing up in a nationally known Italian-American community mean assuming a ready set of character traits that pop culture has assigned to my ethnic group (the mobster's bravura; the *cafone's* extravagance)? Traits that can either be tucked away—or put on parade. Identity as a pact of unity; ethnicity as an accident of geography.

In Bensonhurst, I yearn for the next chance to see a woman

leaning out a half-open window in an old housedress, a cigarette dangling between cracked red lips, offering advice about how to find a neighbor who isn't in. If I can understand the residents of these insular blocks, the largest Italian-American enclave in New York City, denounced by the media as a paradigm of racism and overportrayed by Hollywood; if I can understand a true Italian community, one so opposite from the community in which I grew up, I can, my reasoning suggests, unlock secrets of my inherited identity.

I have made these trips from Manhattan to Bensonhurst, oddly, every seven years over the last two decades. In 1982 and 1989, I went to the neighborhood as a reporter to observe marches organized by the African-American community in protest of two racial murders. First an African-American transit worker named Willie Turks was killed after leaving a midnight shift at a car maintenance yard. Turks had stopped for a snack with some other workers at the Avenue X Bagel Shop in Gravesend, a community that borders Bensonhurst, when their car stalled outside the shop. A gang of about twenty Italian-American teens approached Turks and his colleagues and began throwing bottles, shouting "Nigger, get out of here." Following the charge of an eighteen-year-old gang leader, Gino Bova, they dragged Turks out of his car and beat him to death.

At the end of the decade, a young man named Yusuf Hawkins, from a black section of Brooklyn several miles away, accompanied a friend who was planning to buy a used car in Bensonhurst. Shortly after Hawkins and his friends stepped foot in the predominantly white community, they found themselves surrounded by a group of angry Italian-American males. As another racial tragedy unfolded on that August night in 1989, the protagonist changed from Gino to Gina, a modern-day Circe who had the power of turning good boys into swine.

Residents blamed a young woman named Gina Feliciano of Italian and Latina heritage, who dangerously flirted with a Bensonhurst teenager named Keith Mondello, for sparking the violence. She boasted that her black and Latino friends were coming to celebrate her birthday, and that on that night they would whip the local boys' "pussy white asses." Mondello formed a nighttime posse to defend the neighborhood; and while Gina's threats were false, that fact proved of little use to the young Yusuf Hawkins. The gang thought that Hawkins was one of Gina's pals, and by the time Mondello recognized their mistake, it was too late. A hot-tempered and mentally slow young man named Joey Fama walked up to Hawkins and pulled the trigger of a .32 caliber revolver.

Twice in seven years, the African-American community rallied in southern Brooklyn to mourn the deaths of their own. During these protest marches, I watched dozens of young Italian-American men station themselves in front of the area's one- and two-family homes to defend the sanctity of their neighborhood. The urban warriors stood with their feet apart, arms crossed at the chest. They wore sleeveless T-shirts to show off pumped-up biceps, and jeered, inviting confrontation. Watermelons, the emblem of Bensonhurst anger, were lifted overhead as residents shouted at the protesters.

As I stood behind police barricades, I witnessed generations of entrenched Italian-American hatred: old women shook their heads and muttered in disgust as marchers passed by; young men tried to hurl their bodies past the restraints, the veins on their foreheads bulging like earthworms after a rain. Sickened and terrified that violence would break out on those afternoons, I didn't know what to do. Twice my body responded with the same forceful reflex: I dashed into an Italian bakery.

The smell of sweet butter floated in the air, and I breathed deeply, letting the gentle aroma glide up my nose and penetrate my fear. I surveyed the typical Italian sweets before me: trays of cheesecakes dusted with a snowfall of powdered sugar, pieces of cannoli stuffed with mounds of creamy ricotta, a row of *sfogliatelle* that rested snugly in its crunchy Neapolitan shell. Each time I bought some easy-to-eat pignoli cookies. I longed for their sweet almond paste, a poultice for a throat parched by fear. Confronted with Italian-American racism, I had to offset this detestable part of my culture with a small token of childhood comforts, a familiar taste to prove that there were parts of Italian-American life that provided joy.

After the Hawkins incident, the neighborhood became a national spectacle, and journalists quickly wrote up accounts of racism in Bensonhurst. But I couldn't find any words to fill the blank page. I had pages and pages of interviews, reams of information in my notebook to shield me from false interpretations like a protective amulet, containing the "truth" about people whom I did not know, but with whom I felt an uneasy kinship. As an Italian-American, I was conflicted, unable to articulate my deep embarrassment; as an outsider, I secretly hoped that the neighborhood's unsightly response was a caricature, performed solely for the hordes of television cameras.

Each character in the drama played his part with the skill of the Method actor: reporters looked for the quick sound bite to confirm that Bensonhurst was a cauldron of racial hatred; the Reverend Al Sharpton, New York's vocal minister for racial justice, scheduled several more neighborhood marches to keep the anger brewing between Italian-Americans and African-Americans; and residents continued to jeer and joke about the "moulies," a southern Italian slur for blacks derived from the dialect word *(mulignan')* for eggplant *(melanzana)*.

The brutal honesty of Bensonhurst's public rage kept me spellbound that summer; I had known only private rage. I watched anger erupt and then retreat, the battle ongoing in words alone—no one else was injured on the streets during the long, hot months of marches. I felt the danger of being a modern participant in the complex historical relationship between the southern Italian, whose land borders Africa and was dominated for centuries by dark-skinned Moors, and the black man. At the beginning of the century, olive-skinned southern Italians brought an ambiguous racial identity to their new land, causing a U.S. Senate committee to label them "nonwhite"; and ethnic historians have noted that because Italian-American agricultural workers in the post-Reconstruction South resembled their black coworkers, they were similarly subjected to the restrictions of Jim Crow legislation. Over a hundred years later, the intertwining of olive and chocolate, still threatened the sense of Italian-American wholeness; the Bensonhurst neighborhood fought to maintain its slight tilt toward whiteness on the melatonin scale.

Months after the marches ceased, I packed away my filled notebooks and tape cassettes, unable to draw a cohesive portrait from the scattered bits of information I had collected. I left my job as a journalist to become the chief speechwriter for David N. Dinkins, who many political observers say was elected as New York's first African-American mayor in part because he offered a sense of calm in the aftermath of the Hawkins murder to a racially frayed city. While I wrote many speeches calling for tolerance and racial harmony, to me they were only political speeches, filled with catchwords and phrases that may make people feel good, but that offered little analysis of the complexities of ethnicity and race.

The gap between my mental preoccupation with Bensonhurst and my inability to put those thoughts on paper plagued me, and when I finally returned, seven years after the Hawkins murder, I needed to prove to myself that I could write about the neighborhood. I wanted to understand this urban ethnic culture through the prism of my experience, and I recalled Italo Calvino's definition of experience: "memory plus the wound it has left in you, plus the change it has worked in you that has made you different."

In the portrait of Bensonhurst that emerged after the Hawkins tragedy, Italian-Americans appeared before me like cardboard cutouts, angry, insular, capable of murder, yet I also sensed that many residents were as familiar as family, decent people but with views different from my own. And I became angry, as I do with my own family, at their inability to reason abstractly: yes, they were right to assert that it was a mentally impaired young man who pulled the trigger that killed Hawkins, but they refused to accept blame for an entrenched bigotry that created the setting for this racial tragedy. I needed to discover what traits I shared with these residents because I had made myself the "other," quickly drawing a line between me and them. The nagging question that taunts the suburban ethnic rang in my ears: what is my relationship to my heritage if this community defines Italian-American culture for the rest of us?

"ANTHONY, STOP SCREAMING, ANTHONY. No, I said no. Anthony, I said no. Anthony—stop, stop—stop screeeeeeming!"

Welcome back, I thought to myself, stepping out of the elevated subway in the heart of commercial Bensonhurst at Eighty-sixth Street and Eighteenth Avenue to the jolting sound of a battle erupting between a mother and her young son. It was an emotional outburst typical of a community that announces its intimacy daily. Anthony looked to be about four years old, and he bawled and bawled, plopping himself down on the pavement with the fortitude of a desert monk: there was no chance that his mother could make him walk home. The small, dark-haired woman responded by screaming at a pitch higher than that of the boy's well-practiced wails. My eardrums pulsed as I passed them, and I tried to ignore the scene. By the red traffic light, they were by my side again, miserable Anthony and his miserable mom dragging him down the street.

"This kid is driving me crazy," the mother said, turning to me and cupping her hands to her ears. "He just took his medication and now he wants candy."

"Anthony, that's it. I'm going home. I am leaving you here," she announced in the middle of the next block—a threat that she abandoned a few seconds later.

The little boy looked so forlorn that I remembered his face well even after I had turned the corner and the domestic cries had blended into the roar of a passing subway car. At the time, I was six months pregnant, and wondered in the protective stillness of daydreams what kind of mother I would become. I did not envy this woman's job of getting her son home in the middle of a temper tantrum, but it seemed that she could have responded more gently to the child's plea for candy after taking medication.

After only a few minutes in Bensonhurst, already I longed for the anonymity and comparative quiet of Manhattan's streets. The woman's desire to match her son's shouts was all too familiar to me—this tolerance in Italian-American households of hysterics and exaggerated behavior, the seeming comfort of noise filling the air, screaming as a response to traumas small and large. When, as children, my siblings and I acted out at home, our yelling com-

peted with my mother's high-pitched retorts. There was no discussion, no bribery, no being sent to our rooms. But my parents
chose to live in the suburbs, and that decision meant adapting to
its social decorum. Our rules were simple: we couldn't fight on the
street, and we had to shut the windows at home or else the neighbors would hear.

A word-of-mouth promise of a good place to live sent my
grandparents from New York Harbor to northern New Jersey,
where these immigrants from Conza della Campania and Picerno
settled in small towns near the city of Newark. Only thanks to
this geographic decision did I not grow up as an ethnic among
ethnics in a place like Bensonhurst; instead I had been among the
dark minority in "white" territory.

AT BROOKLYN'S SOUTHERNMOST POINT, Bensonhurst
is nestled between the wealthier Italian-American neighborhoods
of Bay Ridge, which borders New York Harbor, and Dyker
Heights, and to the east the working-class Italian community
of Gravesend. Each section displays its own form of
Italian-American culture, from the gaudy drapery of Christmas
lights adorning Bay Ridge's prosperous homes to Bensonhurst's
salumerias, stocked with shelves of imported pasta and canned
tomatoes. Class, not cultural differences, separates these four
overlapping sections, and I have perceived few differences along
these streets in the attitudes and values of the people.

When I returned to Bensonhurst in the late nineties, all of
the community's familiar fixtures seemed intact since my last
neighborhood pilgrimage: sullen row houses, diners with heavy
plastic menus and revolving pastry wheels, packed pizzerias, cafés
with old men sipping espresso, brick Catholic churches. But cen-
sus experts and neighbors tell me that Bensonhurst is different.
City planners say that from 1980 to 1990, the number of Italian-

Americans living in the area declined by 22 percent, a drop 5 percent larger than in all of New York City, and a trend, they add, that
will continue in the twenty-first century. And that change, in the
parlance of a woman who was born in Sicily and raised her family in Bensonhurst, means: "The neighborhood is going to shit."

Over thirty thousand Russians and Asians have moved into
the community, bringing modest changes to mostly Italian streets.
Wandering into a deli in Gravesend, I found that my lunch choice
was meat-stuffed cabbage instead of the mozzarella and prosciutto that I had craved. While Italian had been the language of
choice for generations along Eighteenth Avenue, Bensonhurst's
largest commercial strip, residents complain that the Asian and
Russian newcomers aren't making a sufficient attempt to speak
English, and merchants even formed an association to ensure that
the signs in front of all stores are posted in English. Despite the
residents' fears about this recent wave of immigration, Bensonhurst is still over 65 percent Italian-American.

Neighborhood people anxious about their future complain
that the streets are no longer safe. "I don't know half the people
around here," said a young woman. "When I was little, I used to
know everyone, and I could play out on the street. My mother
could sit on the porch. It's not the same anymore." This young
woman was unable to articulate why it was less safe for children
to play on the street and her mother to sit on the porch, other
than to explain that the people in the neighborhood were "different."

Changes in the economy and the loss of union protections
have hit this heavily blue-collar community of plumbers, electri-
cians, and construction workers hard. Enterprising immigrants
willing to work for low wages have edged Italian-Americans out
of lifetime jobs. Each morning before dawn, South and Central
American immigrants line up along Eighteenth Avenue to be

picked up by construction crews. Residents don't blame the Italian-American construction companies for demanding the cheapest labor; instead they bitterly complain that "the Mexicans" are stealing their jobs.

Rage has found a secure home under the shingled roofs of Bensonhurst's row houses. To many residents, Bensonhurst's ability to isolate itself and preserve Italian-American culture for generations is its major appeal; when threats to the dominant culture arise, the neighborhood reacts, often violently. In the past few years, more bias crimes have been reported in southern Brooklyn, one of the few remaining white enclaves, than anywhere else in the borough. The community predictably closes in on itself during divisive times, defending its boys as good kids and branding others the enemy.

Xaverian High School, an all-male Catholic school in Bay Ridge, educates the majority of Italian-American young men from the area, charging a tuition of five thousand dollars a year. The public school, New Utrecht, once the alma mater of most Bensonhurst residents, now enrolls primarily a minority population, and while Xaverian offers a more protected environment, no school can isolate students from the lure of the streets.

A Xaverian honors student and altar boy, John Tanico, went to jail for being part of a gang that beat an inebriated Ecuadoran homeless man to death in 1994. Tanico was among a group of Italian-American kids who could no longer hide their resentment that Ecuadorans were using the park, and they drew an imaginary line to divide up the playing field: Ecuadorans (whom Bensonhurst residents in a confused ethnic geography call "Mexicans") were on one side, Italian-Americans on the other. When Tanico hit his handball to the Ecuadoran side and they kicked it back "disrespectfully," he told his friends about the incident and, in a response reminiscent of the feral behavior of the gang that cornered Yusuf Hawkins, the group went back later that night carrying lead pipes, bats, and aluminum lawn furniture. Most of the Ecuadorans fled upon seeing the armed posse, except for one drunk homeless man, who weaved toward them and was beaten to death.

The killing of an Ecuadoran did not generate the widespread press attention of the Hawkins murder. I learned about the incident reading the Metro section of the *New York Times*, and was left with the same sense of dread that I had felt after the Hawkins tragedy: a distorted ethnic pride in insecure times had again produced an anger that led to murder. The following year, two Italian-American teenage brothers from Bensonhurst were arrested after a morning-long rampage; their string of victims included a Central American day laborer waiting on Eighteenth Avenue for construction work, and a sixty-eight-year-old Asian man who was beaten until he lost consciousness.

Around the same time as the Dyker Park incident, several Xaverian students were suspended from school because the lure of organized crime and its promise of easy money cost them nearly ten thousand dollars apiece in gambling debts to local bookies. And when I visited Xaverian a few years later, guided through the labyrinth of youth culture by the school's candid president and chief administrator, Sal Ferrera, the media was inquiring about a student named Jason Andrade, who was charged with beating another youth into a coma during a drunken brawl that erupted a block away from the 1997 St. Patrick's Day parade. Andrade was among a gang of twenty Bay Ridge teenagers who picked a fight with a group of high school students from the Throgs Neck section of the Bronx.

I wondered if the romanticized notion that Italian-Americans exact retribution and balance the scales of justice in the veiled solitude of night fuels the raw anger of Bensonhurst young men who lack aspirations and have looked for models in the larger-than-life figure of the mobster. Ferrera held a parents' meeting at Xaverian about the growing problem of teen violence three weeks after the St. Patrick's Day beating took place, and tragically on the day the assaulted boy died from his injuries. Letters had been sent to thirteen hundred parents asking them to attend, but only about forty showed up. The meeting began with a short prayer, followed by talk about the challenges of raising teenagers in today's violent culture. The parents who filled the first few rows of the large empty auditorium came with different agendas. A few leaned forward in their seats, their faces tight with anxiety and concern, and eagerly raised their hands to discuss youth violence. Others sat together, savoring the social event, gossiping about the different teachers who spoke; one woman was only interested in discussing why there was no intramural baseball team for her son.

While Xaverian is over 80 percent Italian-American, administrators say that most parents show minimal interest in getting involved in their sons' lives at school, believing their responsibility ends as soon as they sign the tuition check. The school thus becomes a distrusted institution, a necessary fact of life, but inferior to the value structure provided by the family.

Even among the many middle-class families from Bay Ridge and Dyker Heights who send their sons to Xaverian, the tuition to attend a top university does not fit into the equation of their life: it's cheaper for their children to attend community colleges, and neighborhood mores urge young men and women to live at home until they marry. At parent-teacher conferences, a father is more likely to ask if his son "shows respect" than to inquire about the curriculum.

Ferrera, who has spent his teaching and administrative career in Bensonhurst and Bay Ridge, explained in a husky voice and a

Brooklyn accent never lost from his youth: "I came up with a term, I call it the 'Mediterranean malaise' that parents have, especially Italian-American parents, that if my son is good and he's not struggling, I don't have to worry about it. To get Italian-American families to understand that they have to achieve and have to push harder," he adds, "that the whole world is open to them, is quite difficult."

A self-employed young man who grew up in Bensonhurst put it this way: "I come from a neighborhood where we thought working on a garbage truck was a good job."

My frustration upon hearing these stories has to do not with our shared experience but with my narrow escape. I was raised by a father who never took us on family vacations because the costs were too high, but who paid in full for the undergraduate and graduate degrees for me and my brother at private universities. No other third-generation women in my extended family had the same experience, and I had the added good fortune of attending highly regarded suburban public schools. In some ways, Bensonhurst has become a kind of repository for my exasperation about certain facets of Italian-American culture. Twenty years after I left home to attend school, the young women I met from Bensonhurst were applying to mediocre local colleges because their parents wanted them to stay by their side.

"Frozen in time" were the words that another Xaverian educator, Nancy Santoro-Heiles, used to describe the culture and values of the young men whom she has instructed. Santoro-Heiles, who heads the school's student exchange program, has lived in Bensonhurst since the 1950s and frequently travels back to the village in Sicily where she was born. In Sicily, she has seen traditions abandoned as her town has gradually absorbed the influence of the dominant, evolving Italian culture. Conversely, southern Brooklyn's Italian-American enclave replicates the past by preserving tradition, producing a culture that Santoro-Heiles believes "has become stagnant, that doesn't allow you to grow."

An immigrant culture by definition can only be maintained through memory and tradition; as the next generation establishes itself in America, the past is seen through the ever more distant lens of grandparents or great-grandparents recalling their place of birth. The immigrants' offspring must adapt to a constantly shifting American landscape, while the Italian culture they have inherited, and that they are forced to reimagine, may be as ancient as the nineteenth-century villages of their families.

All groups use food, language, and memory to preserve their heritage, yet notions about culture can become distorted. Italian-Americans commonly regard themselves as "Italian," treating the latter part of their hyphenated identity as a necessary appendage and lumping together other ethnic groups (Irish, German, English) as "American": "My American friends could go to Florida for Christmas or Thanksgiving," a former Bensonhurst resident told me, recalling her college days and the strict family code dictating that holidays must be spent at home. Many Bensonhurst high school students I met proudly described themselves as "Italian," not Italian-American or American, but they can't speak Italian, making it impossible for them to understand the primary culture they choose to identify with. The dilemma is shared by all hyphenated Americans, bombarded with so many chaotic images from the larger culture that we long for simplicity and a return to the stories and traditions of our parents and grandparents.

Bensonhurst residents, who must confront an evolving ethnic and racial landscape, see change as a mechanism that dilutes and eventually destroys the past. Rage is acceptable, condonable, if it helps to preserve Italian culture. Rage, tangible and heartfelt, replenishes a diminished memory. The future, which can only be imagined through a porous net of hope and fear, remains frighteningly out of reach, lacking, in the words of the writer Giuseppe Di Lampedusa, the "stone and flesh" of the past, "that charge of energy which everything in the past continues to possess."

The residents' decision to shield themselves from others has come at a heavy price. The culture is a mélange of fact and fiction, a result of the struggle that takes place in ethnically insular pockets of American cities. When newcomers arrive on these blocks, the threat is palpable; the wall of isolation crumbles, for Bensonhurst residents' tenuous hold on memory is based on a belief that once upon a time there was bread and wine and boccie and laughter that, without their fortitude and determination, will be lost forever. They are forced to cling to a distant culture they will never fully know.

II. IDENTITY

Hollywood, which loves a dash of ethnic flavor, has made Bensonhurst a fiery locale on the American landscape, casting it with excitable, loveable characters that are embedded in our memory. In the 1950s, Bensonhurst was television's generic working-class community, the home of bus driver Ralph Kramden and his subterranean sewer pal Ed Norton in "The Honeymooners." In 1975, when I was a junior in high school, Bensonhurst's New Utrecht High became the symbolic setting for difficult and remedial students with the television show "Welcome Back, Kotter." Gabriel Kaplan, who wrote and starred in the series, played the teacher Kotter, and based the sitcom on his recollections of growing up in this once primarily Italian-American and Jewish enclave. Filmed in California, "Kotter" opened with the gritty urban landscape that Americans imagine to be New York: a shabby "Welcome to Brooklyn" sign and footage of the run-down, graffiti-filled New Utrecht (although the high school in the series was given another name). The show's borscht-belt humor portrayed Bensonhurst as the home of tough, brainless youths: "I want students, real students," pleaded Kotter, "not hit-men-in-waiting."

"When I'm in that classroom," remarked the sitcom's antediluvian vice principal, "I think of myself as a missionary among savages in New Guinea."

John Travolta made his acting debut as the slow but sweet Vinnie Barbarino, one of Kotter's "Sweathogs" (the nickname for the Special Guidance Remedial Academics Group). He had the soft, empty gaze of a gazelle, and sat at the back of the class churning out Brooklyn witticisms like "Up your nose with a rubba hose." Gabriel Kaplan's well-timed pauses, frizzy black hair, and bushy mustache made him the Groucho to Travolta's Chico.

Travolta, convincing in the part of the sexy dolt, was cast in the 1977 film *Saturday Night Fever* as Tony Manero, an Italian-American trapped in a paint shop during the day who finds his true luster on Saturday nights in the animalistic ritual of disco dance. To the Bee Gees' high-pitched call of "Stayin' Alive," Travolta twirled his narrow hips along the strobe-lit disco floor of the Odyssey, a Bay Ridge nightclub, and helped launch what became known as "the disco decade."

Throughout the eighties, Bensonhurst teens dressed in shiny white and black polyester; and during my visits there I half expected to hear the film's embarrassing dialogue, its subtly phrased lines defining the gender politics of the streets: "You thinking like I'm promoting your pussy, but I ain't." Bensonhurst residents now in their thirties still talk about their teenage days when *Saturday Night Fever* was filmed on these streets, immortalizing on the screen a slice of their lives; and high school students not even born in 1977 tell me that it is one of their favorite movies. And *Fever*'s allure lives on: a musical based on the movie opened in London and came to Broadway in 1999.

Saturday Night Fever was developed from a *New York* magazine article called "Tribal Rites of the New Saturday Night" that profiled the dark Brooklyn ethnic, young men known as "cugines," from the Italian word for cousin, *cugino.* The article, cited among my feature-writing colleagues for years, was a kind of case study of a journalist's good fortune, showing how a colorful piece of reporting can end up as a movie script. Twenty years after the release of *Fever,* however, its author, Nik Cohn, published an unexpected confession in a *New York* magazine issue celebrating the film's anniversary: he had made it all up.

The story was a fake, a "fugazy," as young men from Bensonhurst would say today, mimicking with effortless bluster Al Pacino (also a hero of Tony Manero's) in a more recent film about their neighborhood, *Donnie Brasco,* the tale of a mob informer. Cohn, a rock critic from London who grew up in Northern Ireland, had proposed a feature about how the "have-nots" come alive through disco music, and some not-politically-correct editors awaited the raw cut of Italian-American life that he promised to deliver. But when Cohn reached the Bay Ridge nightclub, he encountered the journalist's thorny dilemma of needing to find a story that fit his original idea.

Included in his mea culpa: "The noise level was deafening, the crush of sweaty bodies suffocating, and none of my attempts at striking up conversations got beyond the first few sentences. . . . Plus, I made a lousy interviewer. I knew nothing about this world, and it showed. Quite literally, I didn't speak the language. So I faked it." He found one animated image and secured it in his memory: "a figure in flared crimson pants and a black body shirt. . . . There was a certain style about him—an inner force, a hunger; and a sense of his own specialness."

Posing as a modern-day Kipling, the journalist described in "Tribal Rites" the primitive life force of the dark other: "black hair and black eyes, olive skin . . . and teeth so white, so dazzling, that they always seemed fake. Third-generation Brooklyn Italian, five-foot-nine in platform shoes." Cohn had imagined, he explained two decades later, "how it would feel to burn up, all caged energies."

The article concluded with hero and friends climbing into an old Dodge—"a posse seeking retribution which was their due, their right"—to hunt down a man who had stared for too long at a neighborhood girl. "*Hombre,* you will die," shouted these "horsemen" as they drove into the dark Saturday night. Cohn's overwritten hoax was set into type, and the editors, who never questioned the author, added an introductory note attesting to its accuracy.

No one in the media took Cohn, or the magazine, to task for his nonchalant confession, already twenty years too late. The author's interpretation of Italian-Americans merely confirmed people's beliefs about the dark working-class ethnic. It didn't matter if the story was made up: the figure of Tony Manero standing before a bedroom mirror in low-cut briefs, a gold cornetta and cross dangling over shiny black hair that fanned his chest and narrowed at the waist to a pencil-thin line tracing down to his pelvis, promised primal heat. What a shame he lacked a brain. He was, and is, how people want to see Italian-Americans, and how many Italian-American young men wish to see themselves. His actions, whether pointing a hand toward the heavens on the disco floor or forming a posse to defend the honor of his neighborhood, have been reenacted by Bensonhurst youth, repeatedly. The real and the fictional community have become intertwined, the participants and observers engaged in a dance where each movement depends upon the cue of the one before.

The popularity of films like *Fever* and a decade later *Moonstruck*, written by an Irish-American charmed by overwrought Italian-American behavior, enlarged this Brooklyn world and reinforced the portrait of the sexy, dumb, high-strung Italian. Similarly, the enormous appeal of the *Godfather* films enabled Gambino crime head John Gotti to adopt a Marlon Brando stature as mob patriarch; he even played the musical score from *The Godfather* at his notorious hangout, the Ravonite social club. Young men in Bensonhurst in search of a career more glamorous than a job on a sanitation crew still emulate the larger-than-life Gotti, who is now serving time in a federal penitentiary. But it's hard to sort out the truth from fiction about the mafia's involvement on these streets.

"The Gambino brothers, with them everybody ate," said thirty-four-year-old Anthony Riccio, who has lived in the Bensonhurst area all his life. "They kept everybody working. They were more fair than the government."

Riccio described how the mafia has changed since his childhood: "They would make a deal, no double-talk. . . . They went into vices, gambling and loan-sharking. They didn't kill people as much as went on in the eighties and nineties."

As an Italian-American whose only knowledge of the mob is through film, I had to suppress a smile because his depiction of the mobsters' transformation from gamblers to drug suppliers seemed straight out of Mario Puzo, and his suggestion of Gambino "fairness" mirrored the opening scene of *The Godfather*. I could imagine the funeral parlor director uttering the movie's famous first line, "I believe in America," and asking Don Corleone for a type of justice that the government failed to deliver. ("Why did you go to the police first?" Don Corleone asks. "Why didn't you come to me?")

"And you knew these men?" I asked Riccio.

"They were always a ghost," he responded, "quiet, no one talked about it. I saw men of honor. I saw it, but I didn't know it."

After years of television and movie portrayals, does Hollywood imitate life or did the mobster and the cugine adopt the traits of their fictional counterparts, mimicking the language and characteristics that have been assigned to Italian-Americans, responding to an offer that they cannot well refuse? In this chicken-and-egg question, it's easy to find the source of artistry for the Brooklyn Italian in the number of films made in which they have been cast as dons or dimwits: *Goodfellas, My Cousin Vinny, Angie, Moonstruck, Jungle Fever,* and *Donnie Brasco,* to name just a few. When Hugh Grant starred in the 1999 film *Mickey Blue Eyes* as an Englishman hoping to gain acceptance into the mob family of his fiancée, the character he played summed up both the Anglo-American affection for and condescension toward Italian-Americans. It's funny to hear a starchy Brit try to mouth "fuhgeddaboutit," but the syllabic slur reminds us that the Brit/the Wasp must struggle to uneducate himself in order to be recast as Hollywood's Italian-American archetype.

My own reaction to these relentless film images recalls Sartre's classic explanation in *Anti-Semite and Jew* of how stereotypes can redefine reality. The victim of stereotyping, Sartre argues, who internalizes the characteristics he is said to possess, attempts to separate himself from the negative image: "They have allowed themselves to be poisoned by the stereotype that others have of them, and they live in fear that their acts will correspond to this stereotype. . . . [T]heir conduct is perpetually overdetermined from the inside." The Jews, according to this circular theory of self-definition, not only wish to adopt the characteristics associated with the Gentiles, "they seek also to distinguish themselves radically from the acts catalogued as 'Jewish.' "

The screen personas force Italian-Americans into a similar no-win position: choose to be a Bensonhurst Italian or an assimilated American, an ethnic champion waving a red, green, and white flag or a communal player hoping against hope to blend into Anglo-Saxon society. The exaggerated behavior of the Bensonhurst Italian-American and the cool distance of his suburban counterpart may clash on the surface, but both share an uncertain sense of self and fierce defensiveness.

IN THE PROTECTED WORLD of Xaverian High School, as students pursue the timeless agenda of wanting to fit in, they know that their neighborhood radiates a Hollywood cachet. Young men boast that when they visit out-of-state friends and family, girls fall for their Brooklyn address, America's modern gangster land of handsome toughs Al Pacino, Ray Liotta, Johnny Depp, and Robert De Niro. The depiction of Brooklyn men as mob thugs is reinforced in the daily banter between students and the adults who supervise them: the lunchtime cafeteria monitor, speaking into a microphone to announce the end of the meal period, tells "Don Corleone" at the back table to keep quiet.

These boys, by nature of their address, are members of an exclusive club: mafia Brooklyn as seen by millions of Americans. Yet those who pursue the story line, adopting the gangland persona and imagining themselves to be players, may wind up in a tragic ending. According to the Manhattan district attorney's office, Jason Andrade, the Xaverian student accused of fatally punching and kicking high school senior Michael Sarti in the head during a drunken street brawl on St. Patrick's Day, was heard telling his bleeding victim words to the effect of: "Look at me. I'm the one who did this to you." Xaverian teenagers pinpointed for me the origins of Andrade's bravura: Chazz Palminteri, playing a mafia tough in *A Bronx Tale*, delivered the line after winning a bloody barroom fight. Sarti remained in a coma on a life-support machine until he died. And in a Hollywood-style conclusion, Andrade was acquitted of all charges after defense lawyers raised a reasonable doubt about who had delivered the fatal blow in this act of gang violence.

To young men, the "guido" (the term that has replaced last decade's "cugine") is the coolest guy in the school. Guidos, according to the stereotype, wear fat silver chains around their neck, blue Fila sneakers, and gel back a thick head of dark hair, sometimes dying blond a wisp that brushes the forehead. To heighten their allure, they are supposedly "connected"—the hazy word that links them to gangsters. "Guidettes," or "bimbettes," are girls with obvious traits that identify them as "Italian": thick Brooklyn accent, bright lipstick, big hair. (Guidos and guidettes take on different names depending on the urban area where they live: the equivalent pair in Newark, New Jersey, and the people I knew growing up, were called "Nicky and Nancy Norkers.")

Dominick, a handsome high school senior who combines a street toughness with a bookish charm, admitted that part of him would like to be the guido, whose studied swagger, steady entourage, and vague association with gangsters draw male admiration and female dates. Yet he hoped to attend an Ivy League school, and realized that the stereotype could haunt him in the future. "They think you're stupid—you're a guido. . . . Maybe they won't give me a job."

Perhaps because men define the role of guido, and the female guidette is merely an appendage to soften truculent maleness, the young women I spoke to were less tolerant of the type: "They're a waste of life," said a college student.

"They're the girls who chew the gum," a high school senior said, loudly imitating the chomping sound. "And all their names are Maria."

"Well, it's nothing bad," another young woman told me. She looked at her friend Angela, with teased hair and a nasal Brooklyn accent. "It's like her," said the girl.

"I consider myself, well, I—I am not a bimbette—but sometimes I do . . ." said Angela, her voice trailing, unable to complete the sentence. She told me later why it's hard to be an Italian-American girl from Bensonhurst: "You're Italian, you're a bimbette. They judge you by your appearance. Meanwhile they don't know what you're like inside."

Angela, who dropped out of New Utrecht High School in her junior year, will probably not, without the tools of education, escape the image of the bimbette. Yet even the young women I met who planned to attend college lacked the ease and self-assurance of their male peers, and defined themselves, like Angela, in terms of what they are not.

"You see, people call me a guinea, but I'm not a guinea," said Annalisa, a senior at a Catholic girls' school in Bay Ridge who was applying to college. "There's a difference. You know how some people call the Irish drunks? There's guineas and there's the Italians."

Annalisa has lived all her life in Bensonhurst with her two brothers and parents, Italian immigrants from Bari and Sicily who run a neighborhood bakery. She was dark-haired and slender, with large brown eyes, yet despite her beauty and graceful manner, she struggled to escape the label of the "guinea."

I asked her to explain this distinction between the Italians and the guineas. We were sitting, along with several other young women and their teacher, in a high school classroom.

"When I look at guineas, they're like—"

"Low-class," interjected her teacher, also an Italian-American whose family came from the south. Guineas are people who don't respect the tradition, the teacher continued. They don't act "like Europeans, which is classic."

"That's right," said Annalisa, following her teacher's prompting. "That's what my mother once told me: 'You're not a guinea—guineas are low-class.' My Irish friends call me a guinea and a greasy Eye-talian. They're joking and everything."

Annalisa explained that her taste is for fairer, blond-haired and blue-eyed men. She only likes Scottish and Irish boys, which does not please her mother. "Marry within your own," her mother advises. "Your customs are easier."

Already Annalisa has intuited the stigma attached to the dark ethnic. While she may not be able to escape this judgment because of her looks and background, she can find a more comfortable place in the world through her taste and choice in men. No one tells her that "guinea" is an unacceptable word; rather, the image keeps reappearing on television and movie screens, reinforcing the idea that to be a guido, like being gay, does not involve choice but is a lifestyle determined at birth. Annalisa's teacher helps her make these distinctions, suggesting that "good" Italian-Americans act like Europeans, a silly analogy since, more than likely, her ancestors were southern Italian peasants who had little in common with the "classic" European of the woman's imagination.

At a very young age, Bensonhurst Italians are judged to be guidos. Sal Ferrera said that the identity of the young people whom he has educated was fundamentally shaped by their experiences growing up in this Italian-American enclave. As a teacher, he saw how some colleagues refused to enhance an elementary school curriculum because "they believed these kids were going to be bricklayers"; as an assistant principal, he watched on his first day as a teacher disciplining a fourth grader called him a "grease-ball"; and as the head of Xaverian, he still challenges the low expectations that parents have for their children.

"When I was in seventh grade, they put all the Italians on one side," explained a woman who grew up in Bensonhurst, describing how the Italian-American girls were relegated to home economics classes while "the Jewish girls took honors English." The woman, who was part of a 1985 "enthnotherapy" group formed by psychologist Aileen Riotto Sirey to explore the issue of low self-esteem among Italian-Americans, explained to the other participants that she was one of the few Italian-American girls considered "bright"—a label that tracked her with the Jewish girls and ultimately led her to abandon the friends assigned to the home ec and commercial courses.

Bensonhurst residents are compelled to engage in a "contest for dignity," as Richard Sennett and Jonathan Cobb astutely observed in their classic study of ethnics in Boston, *The Hidden Injuries of Class.* Instead of looking at the injustices within the system that impede their academic and social growth, people judge one another. If others can't ascend the class ladder, they say, it's their fault, not ours.

When I travel to Bensonhurst, I too use the armor of class distinction to separate myself from the stereotype of the Brooklyn Italian. My middle-class suburban background, regional Northeastern accent, and university education reinforce an impulse to remain separate, rather than to seek common ground with other Italian-Americans. If residents behave badly, as they did after the Hawkins murder, I am embarrassed, but tell myself that I was raised better. Like many who covered the Hawkins trial and who organized the marches, I can make Bensonhurst an open target, an example of Italian-American behavior at its worst.

Yet it's a terrible trade-off to think of oneself as a different kind of Italian-American than someone like Angela, who is trying to find a place in the shadows of a male-dominated community because she physically embodies the "bimbette"; or to join Italian-Americans in secretly judging each other, watching, assessing, hoping to suppress marks of ethnicity because our concept of dignity has no place for the low-class Bensonhurst Italian.

III. RACE

In Spike Lee's 1989 film *Do the Right Thing*, audiences met another type of Bensonhurst Italian, the explosive racist whose IQ is set at room temperature. *Do the Right Thing* takes place on a brutally hot day at Sal's Famous Pizzeria in the black Bedford-Stuyvesant section of Brooklyn. Sal (Danny Aiello), an Italian-American from Bensonhurst, runs the pizzeria (or "peesseria," as he pronounces it) along with his two sons, Pino and Vito. Pino, played by John Turturro, who often portrays combustible Mediterraneans, spends his days taking telephone orders and making cracks about the "moulie" neighborhood; he is the archetype of the Bensonhurst and Gravesend youths who held up watermelons during the marches for racial justice. (A decade after making *Do the Right Thing*, Lee cowrote and directed *Summer of Sam*, a film that again reflects the director's penchant for depicting Italian-American men as dumb thugs.)

A conversation takes place in Sal's Famous between the delivery boy Mookie (Spike Lee) and Turturro's Pino that lets both men clumsily reveal the depths of their racial hatred and mutual envy. Surrounded by cheap watercolors of Rome and pictures of famous crooners and hitters like Sinatra and DiMaggio, Mookie, angered by the absence of black faces, asks Pino to name his favorite stars. Pino mentions Magic Johnson, Eddie Murphy, and Prince. When asked how he can admire these black men but hate the African-Americans in the neighborhood where he works, an appalled and confused Pino responds, "They're not niggers. I mean they're not black. Let me explain myself—they're black, but they're not really black."

"Pino, don't deep down inside you wish you were black?" says Mookie, suggesting that the olive-skinned, kinky-haired man resents his African-American nemesis because he resembles him. "You know what they say about dark Eye-talians."

When Bensonhurst residents talk about the origin of their families, they indiscreetly acknowledge that darker shades of skin are found deep in Italy's southern tip: "Some people told me I'm black because I'm part from Sicily," said Annalisa, whose skin contains the yellow-green hues of the south. "My uncle who is Irish teases me and says, 'Sicily is not a part of Italy. That's the crap that the boot's about to step on.'"

In Italy the southerner is the symbol of the uneducated "other," dark as the earth he labored; and recent political movements like the Lombard League have legitimized northerners' anger toward the south by claiming that the impoverished Mezzogiorno is draining resources from the heavily taxed north. The northern judgment that southerners are responsible for their own poverty echoes the generations-old American lament against blacks on welfare.

Italian films, routinely dubbed because of a national distaste for subtitles, provide a useful looking glass into the northern prejudice. The American comedy *Airplane*, for example, the classic parody of action disaster movies, contains a well-known scene in which two African-American men talk in an incomprehensible "jive" to a confused flight attendant trying to give emergency directions. A grandmotherly white woman cheerfully comes to the rescue, letting the attendant know that she speaks the street language and can interpret it. In the Italian version, the jive is dubbed as a southern Italian dialect. (The throaty voice of the American mobster in Woody Allen's 1994 film *Bullets over Broadway* was also dubbed into southern dialect.) In the northern Italian imagination, southerners are close kin to the black man.

When Bensonhurst residents proudly displayed "Italia" T-shirts and bumper stickers during the tense racial marches in the neighborhood, flaunting their ethnic pride and loyalty to the mother country, they missed an irony of their ancestry: these offspring of southern Italians mocked blacks by declaring their allegiance to Italy, a country where northern Italians refer to the land below Rome as "the Africa of Italy." But layers of irony are better left for novels, not real life, which would mean introducing messy contradictions into a tailored version of reality. If family members express a dismay that an Italian-American they know married a black person, and I try to mention the plight of the southern Italian, I am met with confused stares: we can pity *paesans* thought of as black, but what does your point have to do, they ask, with the shame of intermarriage?

My mother has described her father as a compassionate, open-minded man who welcomed his black workers into their apartment for food and drink. "My father always said, 'Everybody has a mouth,' " she'd tell me. Yet there was a catch: my grandparents set aside "separate cups" for the black workers to drink from.

But because of my mother's life circumstances—her "individual experience," as Isaiah Berlin characterized the play of events that shape the self, "the ordinary day-to-day succession of private data which constitute all there is—which are reality"—she perceived that people mocked her son Henry for his mental disabilities, and harbored a great sympathy for the societal underdog. My mother shared this quality with me through the books she avidly borrowed from the public library when I was young. Each week I'd survey her choices: *The Autobiography of Malcolm X*; *Black Like Me*, the story of John Howard Griffin, a white man who chemically altered the color of his skin through injections to learn about racial oppression; *Soul Sister*, a white woman's bad imitation of *Black Like Me*; and *Down These Mean Streets* and *Savior, Savior, Hold My Hand* by the Latino writer Piri Thomas were among her favorites. She would repeat anecdotes from the memoirs, such as how Malcolm had to suffer the pain and humiliation of using lye to straighten his hair. By the time I was eleven, I had read most of these books and made civil rights my personal issue. I once asked my fifth grade teacher if I could read a passage from a Robert Kennedy speech, which I had found in a college book of my brother's, to provoke a discussion on racism. The teacher agreed, but after I finished the excerpt the class sat silently, except for one child who said that he didn't like the "coloreds"; their reaction prompted the teacher to dismiss us for an outdoor recess, and to my utter embarrassment, the other children let out a whoop of joy.

Growing up in a community where Italian-Americans were the ethnic minority, I had to make a choice: conform to a majority vision or sympathize with a minority status. I chose the latter, except the minority I sympathized with was not Italian-American but African-American. My background put me doubly at odds with Bensonhurst residents: I both wanted to extricate myself from their (our) identity as Italian-Americans and felt ashamed of their (our) complicated history with race.

THE RACIST PIZZA MAKER in *Do the Right Thing* admits that his heroes are black, and this same fascination with African-American popular culture exists today among young Italian-Americans in southern Brooklyn. The "tribal rites" of Saturday nights in the nineties are spent in Brooklyn clubs that play rap and hip-hop; either rap or electronic dance—"techno" music from the British new wave, which Bensonhurst young men call "guinea music"—fills the room. Yet the admiration of black culture stops with the stereophonic sound. If a group of African-American men were to show up at one of these all-white clubs, the scene, at best, would be uncomfortable, at worst explosive.

In an odd combination of ethnic admiration and hatred, African-American rappers also imitate the gangster image of Italian-Americans. In 1996 Snoop Doggy Dog released *Tha Doggfather*—which would climb to number one on the pop charts—with the album cover copying the look of *The Godfather*; rapper Percy Miller, known as Master P, cut a 1998 album called *Da Last Don*, and released an independent film of the same title to promote it. Rappers Refugee Allstars showed the timeless cross-cultural allure of *Saturday Night Fever* with their version of the Bee Gee's "Stayin' Alive." Method Man, a member of the Wu-Tang Clan, black hip-hop artists from Staten Island, speaks Italian on the favorite radio station of Xaverian youth, WKTU. Within the self-confined music world of mutual distrust and respect, Italian-Americans admire the cool of hip-hop while black rappers appropriate parts of Italian-American pop culture as their own. The imitation of things Italian-American, and likewise the fascination with African-American style (today the cool of rap, yesterday the cool of jazz), hints at the similarities between both groups. John Gennari, an American studies professor at the University of Colorado, argues that the smoothness of Rat Packer Frank Sinatra with his revolving set of pretty girls influenced the I-always-get-me-some attitude of today's gangsta rappers. Gennari suggests a shared "glandular" sensibility: "earthiness, sensuality, emotional expressiveness, an unembarrassed love of the body."

This closeness to Africans, physically, geographically, and

emotionally, haunts Italian-Americans, especially in ethnic enclaves like Bensonhurst, where their tiny island of isolation is gradually shrinking. Little has changed in the attitude of the neighborhood toward blacks since the Hawkins killing a decade ago. When I asked if it was safe for an African-American to walk the streets of Bensonhurst today, the resounding response was "No."

"You would think there's a law against it or something," a young woman told me, describing the rules of the all-white Eighteenth Avenue.

At a private school like Xaverian, administrators attempt to make the small number of black students feel at home, offering all-day workshops on race relations and inviting former Mayor David Dinkins to speak, yet the lunchroom scene of African-Americans sitting at two tables while Italian-Americans fill up the rest of the large cafeteria makes plain the state of social interaction, and why at least one African-American felt he had to transfer. He had dared to date an Italian-American woman from the neighborhood, the sister of one of his classmates, and feared for his safety.

Suburbanites who hide in gated communities, and who use their distance from cities to ensure that encounters with minorities are chance events, have the luxury of filtering raw emotions. Meanwhile, Bensonhurst's working classes lay their rage on the streets like a protective tarpaulin; the failure to earn a decent education, the loss of union jobs, the further slide down the economic ladder mean that Italian-Americans in Bensonhurst do not believe that they have moved beyond minority status, and feel cheated of daily comforts and deprived of material success. Like their ancestors, they are haunted by the specter of the black man, who is perceived as a threat to their place in society.

"I took an entrance exam for Brooklyn Technical High

School and I scored in the gray area—in the seventies," said Anthony Riccio, who lost his job as a computer salesman after his company was downsized, and now runs his own small trucking business. "But because of affirmative action, I got rejected and the kid lower than me gets extra points. Who knows what my life would have been like if I went to that school?" he said, clutching the memory of a rejection nearly twenty years old.

Not only in Bensonhurst have Italian-Americans complained that they are falling behind in wages and promotions. In 1992 Italian-American professors from the City University of New York filed a lawsuit against the institution, arguing that they had routinely been discriminated against and denied a series of promotions because of their ethnic background. An African-American judge ruled in their favor and sought to remedy the situation. Today the university sends a voluntary "self-identification" form to applicants seeking jobs at its campuses throughout the city. The card lists five groups of "protected classes" that will be specially considered for affirmative action:

American Indian/Alaskan Native
Asian/Pacific Islander
Black
Hispanic (includes Puerto Rican)
Italian American

Over a century after Italian immigrants settled in New York, a federal court judge decided that their descendants who applied for work in the City University system could seek protections awarded to minorities, a unique approach to addressing inequalities given Italian-Americans' uneasy history with race. It seems jarring, or at least out of kilter with textbook theories of assimilation, that one hundred years later, a group of Italian-Americans in the premier urban melting pot, many holding doctoral degrees, went to court to document their struggle to integrate into American society, asking to be included in the category of Americans considered "nonwhite."

In Bensonhurst, residents lambaste other ethnic groups who, they say, unfairly receive government aid. They angrily denounce affirmative action, declaring that they have been forgotten. Yet the City University case makes clear that Italian-Americans who have the wherewithal to organize can earn the modest recompense awarded to those at the bottom of the economic heap, and that at least some will take it if offered.

SOME YEARS AGO, WHEN I moved to the Park Slope section of Brooklyn, a friend of my mother's mentioned that she was perplexed by my decision. "Why would Maria move to Brooklyn?" she asked. "We moved to Short Hills to get out of Brooklyn."

Brooklyn was the place where my family never lived but had to leave. (And I, too, left for Manhattan after only a year in the gentrified Park Slope.) When I first traveled to Gravesend and Bensonhurst in 1982, I encountered boundaries I had already drawn—boundaries excluding the young men who had picked up watermelons to denounce the black marchers, young men matching my idea of the Brooklyn Italian: they had the intelligence of Kotter's Sweathogs and the sculpted body of *Saturday Night Fever's* Tony Manero. I was sixteen when I watched John Travolta play Vinnie Barbarino in "Kotter," and Travolta's character made me want to distance myself from Italian-Americans; to me, he was too stupid to be sexy. Instead, I liked the wit of the Jewish Gabriel Kaplan, a preference that I would maintain in my choices of men later in life. In high school I recognized the Barbarino model in the "Ginzo Gang." Bensonhurst, without my understanding its symbolic role, became an ethnic measuring stick—one that I refused to be judged against.

As part of the New York media, I had to separate myself from the image of the Bensonhurst Italian in order to be taken seriously; this anxiety led to a paralysis in writing about the Yusuf Hawkins murder. Each time I traveled to Bensonhurst, I remained the frustrated outsider, trying to understand a community without ever having spent a night there and waking up the next morning along with its members. I talked to saleswomen in shopping malls, ate focaccia in people's homes, wandered high school halls, visited a center for at-risk teenage girls, ordered lunch at local diners, caught my breath in bakeries. Each time I experienced a familiar unease, meeting people who could be my relatives, and who reminded me that our differences had less to do with character than with geography and education: I was taught by other ethnic groups how to look and act American, or, more to the point, how not to look and act like a Brooklyn Italian.

The fictitious Tony Manero glowed larger-than-life, and he has become relentlessly imitated, real. Young people in search of the part already written have the luxury of choosing from a tireless assortment of Hollywood's Brooklyn. Young high school men think acting the Brooklyn tough will serve them well with the opposite sex; young women who follow these men must accept the self-degradation that accompanies the moniker "bimbette." Yet even the slow-witted Tony Manero knew that there was more to life than hanging off the Verrazano Bridge guzzling beer and strutting on the disco floor. *Fever* ends with a long predawn subway ride to Manhattan in which Tony emerges from the dark tunnels of Brooklyn into the light of the new day; the Hollywood hero can begin his transformative journey by severing himself from his working-class past.

Growing up in the suburbs, I followed the cues of my assimilated counterparts, yet the pain for me was probably no greater than what young women from Bensonhurst experience, as they are expected to live up to the image of the traditional Italian woman. I traveled to Bensonhurst to understand a more "authentic" Italian-American community; but ethnic truth is a muddy conceit, and in America often beheld through the ersatz.

Faith

I S THERE SUCH A THING as an Italian-American God? A way of seeing and believing that is a part of a shared history; a faith that is culturally distinct and filled, perhaps, with as much cynical verve as the dialect we speak? I was considering these questions when I was leafing through a book of Italian dialect poetry in the library and came across a nineteenth-century Neapolitan verse called " 'N paraviso," "In Paradise." The poem, written by journalist and poet Ferdinando Russo, tells the story of a man who soars from the dreariness of earth to the crystal gates of heaven, hoping to witness the glories that await him after death. Relying on a translation—Russo's Neapolitan dialect bore no resemblance to the words I knew—I was struck by the similarity in spirit between the poet, who would have been a contemporary of my paternal grandfather, and the irreverent attitude of the men in our family toward faith.

In this odd tale of unruly saints whose carping about paradise is worthy of a borscht-belt routine ("Always clouds, and this incense making all those fumes!"), the poem culminates with a discussion between the earthly man and heavenly Saint Anthony about the afterlife. To the man's surprise, the old hermit takes the glow off the halo: "We up here," he explains, "are annoyed to have to stay here day after day!"

> *"So here everything is just*
> *like down there?" I said.*
> *"Be smart, my boy,*
> *It's just the same!*
>
> *Why, you think that only*
> *on earth, where you live,*
> *such things happen?*
> *Jesus!"*

The saint passes on tidbits such as "Saint Clement is jealous of Saint Pascal" and "Saint Aloysius is a scoundrel." Only the Madonna is just and good, he proudly concludes, reaffirming the traditional Latin cult of the Virgin. The poem undermines the notion of paradise by suggesting a place where, heaven forbid, tempers flare. Yet the verse need not be read as a jab at the Catholic faith and its belief in a glorious heaven. The flip side of this tale is that Italians are so close to their communion of saints that they intimately know their foibles and are poised to pick out the storms brewing behind the billowy white. Who better than family to speak honestly about family?

Italians are a capricious lot, clutching onto saints and dismissing them with equal drama. The poem's decidedly gruff tone recalls men like my self-declared pious uncle who swore up and down that he had obeyed every commandment—except the one about adultery; or the uncle who made funny faces in a funeral-parlor mirror to ensure that my respectful father would break out in a paroxysm of laughter. These men played with faith, letting the women, the madonnas, be the standard-bearers of devotion, but never abandoned their religion. Men could be scoundrels like Saint Aloysius and of course be forgiven for their sins—as long as the women did the praying for them.

My grandmother called upon a variety of saints, represented by a collection of small approachable plaster statues in blue gowns and brown robes with knotted belts and sad, knowing faces that invited susurrant prayer. Her dresser was her private place of worship, her altar. On it, votive candles flickered in ruby red glass, and statues of Mary, Saint Joseph, and Saint Anthony cast a quiet calm alongside several crucifixes.

The solitary chants of this solemn woman expressed a devotion that would have disturbed the American Irish Catholic hierarchy, which was suspicious of the southern Italian attachment to saints. The peasants' mystical intimacy with their icons threatened the authority of the local parish priest, who was for the Church the sole intermediary between the people and the divine. When my grandmother died, she left behind not only her plaster confidants but a means of worship that seemed eerily excessive compared to the religious practices of 1960s America: the tidy, once-a-week trip to mass.

Many of her saints were divided up between me and my brothers; I inherited several statues of Mary, while my brothers took the male saints and the candles, preserving the remainder of the melted wax by refusing to light the tired wicks. These staunch protectors still line the dressers, our rooms perfectly kept shrines to childhood years, except there is no longer a misty circle on my mirror behind the saint's head, the moist ring formed by the warm breath of a nightly kiss.

Memory is fragile, and I can recall few things about my ma-

ternal grandmother, the only grandparent I briefly knew; the rest
is supplied by stories from my mother that provide a glimpse
into her world. Bedridden for years, and always tired and unwilling to communicate with a little girl, my grandmother died when
I was five. A window into my family's past has been shut by life's
dictates, taking my grandparents before they could form a sil-
houette in my mind, and my imagination has suffered as a result.
But trying to remember my grandmother and observing a certain
otherworldiness in my great-aunts, as a child I began to suspect
that I was part of a mystical, dark, and complex brood that continually invoked God in everyday life, seeking miracles and other
favors.

My grandmother's faith included a predisposition to pre-
monitions. To the rest of the family's dismay, her forebodings
usually arrived during summer vacations at the New Jersey
seashore and forced her husband and children to pack up early—
although they wondered if her sense of doom was related to a
strong distaste for the yearly two weeks of imposed leisure. Once,
receiving a signal that something was wrong in the apartment
building that my grandfather owned, she insisted that the family
return home just a few days after their arrival. They abandoned
the misty ocean air for the solemn ride north, my grandfather's
Model T Ford packed with silent recriminations because no one
ever directly challenged my grandmother's authority. Back home,
the family walked into a small basement flood, the dank cellar
floor tinted majestic purple. My Uncle George had left open the
taps to several barrels of wine—a lesson to either watch George
more closely or take my grandmother's supernatural signals more
seriously.

My mother, for a while at least, adopted an American religious practice that didn't involve worship of a host of saints.
Hers was a Protestant-like belief that could be summed up in a

line: Why ask all those saints for intervention when you can go straight to the top? Unlike the poet, my mother didn't believe that life was bad at the top, but she did harbor a suspicion that a panoply of saints were mediocre intermediaries when big prayers needed big answers.

The third in line of these women, and most inclined to emotional despair over religion's complexities and Church doctrines, I continually feel the tug between a spiritual sense and a maddening frustration over the notion of infallible dogmas and the wagging fingers of papal condemnations. I was raised to believe in a religious relativism that my mother denies she taught me, so I wonder if perhaps I thought it up myself, sitting in the church balcony on those Sundays when the first-floor pews were already taken, experiencing alternating moments of vertigo and high-flying ease. The message I received either from my mother or during those lucid, latitudinarian moments was that a child merely assumed the religion of the family she was born into. No church or temple was superior: the one you attended was a matter of chance.

Those thoughts laid the groundwork for my religious sensibility, and that is why the suspicion and affirmation of the Neapolitan poem appeal to me. I get to ponder otherworldly redemption and snicker at pious hypocrisy. But rather than holding myself culpable for my beliefs, I prefer to think that I've inherited a distrust of the institutional Church, that an atavistic keeper opened the floodgate of my doubts. My grandmother's dresser was as close to God as any official altar, and my mother offered a relaxed approach toward our weekly attendance of Sunday mass.

I usually accompanied my mother, not my father, to church on Sunday mornings. My father, meticulous about every aspect of his life, was always on time: he arrived in the church lot promptly at 9:23, and searched for a space that wouldn't require any difficult maneuvers because he hated parking, which left just enough time to find a seat for the 9:30 mass. While normally a practitioner of solitude, he surprised us by becoming involved in church affairs. For many years he was the secretary of the Holy Name Society, a post that was incomprehensible to me because I assumed that only women were secretaries and was baffled about the role of a society with such a blessed title. Shouldn't only priests be involved in sacred matters?

My mother, on the other hand, made churchgoing her own private affair with a singular set of rules. She waited until the last mass of the day at 12:30, and usually arrived between fifteen to twenty minutes late for the forty-five-minute gathering, which meant skipping the introductory remarks, song, and readings from Scripture, entering midway in the priest's homily. Before mass began, she had brunch to make and dishes to clean and the floor to sweep, and no task could wait until later that day (she joked that by nature she was Martha, not Mary). No matter how much my father—the sole family driver, impatiently pumping the brakes in our driveway—complained about her lateness, she would brush off his disapproval with an all-encompassing "Oh, God will forgive me." I thought her declaration made perfect sense, and also liked to have twenty minutes shaved off church time, so I opted for late sleep and 12:30 mass.

Sunday school was another weekly duty until I reached the confirmation age of twelve. I wiggled and slouched, drew circles with my finger along the small wooden desk, touching its cold steel frame for a moment's diversion—a moist tingle of doubt rocking the cradle of certainty—as the nun quizzed us on the catechism. Catholic teaching when I was growing up was primarily devoted to learning Church rules, basic biblical stories, and the different gradations of sins, rather than engaging children in the humanistic message of the Gospels. I would sit at my desk and look at the clock, and had to be bribed into correctly responding to the lesson.

"I have gifts, you know, for children who answer questions correctly," one nun said with resigned desperation. "Can anyone name one of the gifts delivered to the baby Jesus?"

My listless hand shot up.

"Myrrh," I responded, winning a set of rosary beads.

Religious instruction came from neighbors as well as nuns, and an early prayer I learned is still vivid in my memory. Our next-door neighbor, a kind but strict teacher and devout Irish Catholic who saw my religious upbringing as part of her duty, taught me this bedtime ditty: "Matty, Matty, Luke, and John, / Bless this bed that I lay on. / If I die before I wake, / Pray the Lord my soul to take." I quickly memorized the prayer, although it seems that I must have inadvertently dropped one of the evangelists, Mark, from the group. I had no concept of who these men were, despite the very familiar terms I was on with Matthew. The prayer upset me and reinforced an unconscious terror that I still possess today toward Catholicism and its reliance on death as the passage to redemption. I was about six, too young to think about dying before I went to sleep each night; I wanted to live in a protected world, lulled into the dreamy night.

Today I carry with me the notion that happiness is illusory, a sleight of hand that disappears in the master's grip and surrenders to suffering, the more noble form of life, or, in my relatives' words, the cross that we all must bear. Yet I'm not sure if these beliefs are the by-product of church teaching, a peasant tradition, family circumstances, or a trifecta win of all three. I do know, though, that the simple act of arriving late for church was an antidote to the terror that I felt when inside the imposing religious structure. My mother's willingness to be the last parishioner helped alleviate some guilt and fear by allowing me to conceive of a Catholic faith in which rules were allowed to be broken.

I would describe my family as devout Catholics—even more so today, now that my parents are old: after my father retired he went to church every morning; my brother Bob heads the group of lectors for Sunday mass; my mother quotes Scripture from memory. Yet still, I grew up with a small but lingering sense of distrust about the institutional Church that I've never lost. Perhaps the roots of these doubts are as remote as ancient history: southern Italian peasants have had a long tradition of anticlericalism. If my mother, in part, had intuited her ancestors' blend of faith and skepticism, she saw firsthand that the Church could disappoint, given the injustices done to her son Henry; and her own faith was scarred but never lost. Meanwhile, her two frequently repeated stories—of how a priest mocked her mentally retarded son when he received his first Holy Communion; and of how, with a nun's help, she snuck Henry into confirmation training because the priest in charge refused to admit him—left an indelible imprint on me.

I can imagine the day of my brother's first Communion, how his tongue must have wagged a little too long, the circular paper-thin white host precariously balanced, which prompted the priest to announce harshly, "Stick your tongue in." The curiosity and confusion my brother must have experienced that morning, trying to comprehend the meaning of this hand of authority, the tasteless wafer, and the repeated command, would seem a natural response for slow children and analytical adults alike. Yet both have a difficult time finding a place and acceptance within a conservative Church.

These stories took place inside a church I never attended, in a town I don't remember; my parents moved to Short Hills when I was one, and they never looked back. The priests in our local parish were mostly kind and helpful; some would become mentors to Bob. But I grew up acutely aware of appearances, that deceptive guarantor of approval denied to Henry. The people my parents knew from the town of Millburn, the Italian-Americans from the old neighborhood, sat in the back rows, veiled heads bowed, fingering rosary beads. These ladies in mournful black, vestiges of a nineteenth-century southern Italian culture, understood the social order as intimately as their prayers. The wealthy Irish-American parishioners, the majority in our church, wore bright prints and self-assured smiles, and mingled with each other in the front pews. Where did we fit in? Probably somewhere in between, in those middle rows where we sat by ourselves. The equality we were all supposed to experience in the eyes of God never reached those pews; the working-class women in the back accepted their place and remained there week after week.

The most effective religious instruction of my teenage years came cleverly disguised in the form of an off-Broadway play. I saw a production of *Godspell* in New York, and when the national company came to our local New Jersey theater, I arranged, as a vaguely embarrassed member of the Catholic Youth Organization, to invite the cast to a postmatinee party of six-foot submarines and sodas in our church meeting room. I sent them a note that recast the lyrics to one of the show's songs, a derivation of the "Matty, Matty" rhyme scheme. It went something like this: "Why don't you come and be at ease / leaving when you please / and it won't cost you no money / Come and have a snack / then you go right back / ready to act in your next show. . . ." Surprisingly, they sang the insipid lyrics to each other backstage, and all but one cast member came to the party. Soon I was sending fan letters to several actors, who never responded to my careful pages of script despite the many months I lingered by the mailbox, certain of their reply.

While a girlish crush on actors doesn't constitute a religious experience, or at least a sanctified religious experience, *Godspell* had a larger effect on me. The play was based on the Gospel of Saint Matthew, and when I effused about the show to a neighbor, she suggested I read that Scripture. Despite many years of Sunday school, the Church never encouraged its parishioners, young or old, to read the Bible; and coming across the Beatitudes for the first time, I saw the groundwork for a personal faith. The passage's call for a gentle, humane view of life, its reversal of the social order which could allow our family's last sheep to be first, made more sense to me than the rules I had been taught. A decade later, when an old friend suggested that we see a revival of *Godspell*, I went eagerly. Time and age revealed the feebleness of the production (along with the rude shock that the actor playing Jesus was younger than we were), but for a sixteen-year-old, song and dance, the Gospel and Psalms put to music, were perfect vehicles for spirituality. And while I was always eager for an excuse to miss weekly mass, thanks to free tickets from a friendly box-office worker, I saw the Sunday matinee of *Godspell* seventeen times.

I was more at ease in becoming a *Godspell* groupie than in showing similar devotion to a saint, which put me at odds with my mother, who decided to take up a more mystical form of devotion. My mother had a few good friends, all earnest and supportive companions in her search for the sacred. Most of these women were office colleagues, except for one, a friend from church whose religious quests took her as far as Hong Kong, where she worked on obtaining a patent for her prized invention, dashboard rosary beads. While I never saw the device, I believe it resembled an abacus, allowing the driver to slide a bead, recite a quick Hail Mary, and make a right on red.

I first remember being included in these spiritual quests when a coworker handed my mother a religious pamphlet on Saint Theresa, the unassuming girl whose powers of sainthood included answering prayers with "a shower of roses." The French nun Thérèse of Lisieux was in many ways a perfect saint to capture the imaginations of housewives and single mothers who worked as typists to earn money for their families. Saint Theresa took pride in her ability to perform ordinary female chores to perfection, and she studiously followed, from the age of fifteen, when she became a nun, until her early death at twenty-four, the rigorous Carmelite life.

Saint Theresa believed that it was not through great deeds but through the "little way" of her acts that God's love could be obtained. She would pay meticulous attention to sweeping up cobwebs in the convent, pulling out garden weeds, and diligently sewing despite eyestrain, finding each task as important as her fervent desire to save souls through an unflinching devotion to God. Because my mother dedicated herself daily to small acts, beating out dust from floor mats, planting tulips for the early spring, replacing lost buttons on shirts, the little ways of the nineteenth-century saint had found their way into our house.

But I doubt my mother was aware of the content of Saint Theresa's humble life, which the "little flower" recorded in a journal that would later become her autobiography; I think what appealed to her most was the idea that answered prayers could be confirmed by the appearance of roses. She was moving away from her American suspicion of saints to embrace the mysticism of her ancestors, and was hoping for a tangible response.

"See any roses today?" my mother would ask, hoping to be surprised by a yes. We were supposed to pray to Saint Theresa and wait: perhaps a rose would bloom in a garden deadened by frost, or we'd find one lying along the road, dropped from a bouquet to take on a new life, the sign of Saint Theresa's attentive ear. How do I convey the seriousness of this search? I think my mother, who put tremendous faith in written documents, as if the printer's ink were truth itself, wanted to believe the pamphlet. I tried to make light of the hunt, sighing at the latest antics of my mother and her friends—although I do remember looking for the long-stemmed reward out of the corner of my eye, yearning to receive a heavenly sign.

I remembered this years later when I interviewed the director Nancy Savoca about her film *Household Saints*, which she adapted from the novel by Francine Prose. *Household Saints* is the story of a young girl named Theresa who grows up in Little Italy, a place where magic occurs in making sausage, and fate is decided by a deck of cards (dealt by God, of course). So it's inevitable that Theresa will imitate the harsh life of, and eventually come to resemble, Saint Thérèse. Savoca's interest in making this film stemmed from the touch of magic realism that bloomed in her household from the marriage of her Argentine mother and Italian-American father. "There was the world—what you could see," Savoca explained, "and then there was what you couldn't see, and you always respected that other force that was moving in your life." A butterfly signaled an important letter was coming; a mirror broke, a relative died—the events, of course, were related.

My mother, too, acknowledged this mysterious force, incorporating the inexplicable and the rational, intimately asking God for favors, looking for signs in daily life, complaining loudly when prayers went unanswered. After a few months without seeing a single blossom, we lost interest in this scented search and dropped Saint Theresa from our daily conversations. Still, my fondness for roses remains today; their dark, luxurious petals decorate my Christmas tree, dried and wise among the branches of a young evergreen.

Religion in our household took on different shapes, with seasonal changes usually ushered in with the encouragement of a friend. After Saint Theresa came evangelicalism; my mother routinely began to use language like "being touched by the Holy Spirit." Pat Robertson, Oral Roberts, Robert Schuller, and Jerry Falwell became household names; the "700 Club" broadcast its worldviews into our living room daily. The religious vehemence of evangelicalism threw me off-balance; I had never seen my mother so caught up in a movement that I found threatening and dangerous. For seemingly endless years, we heard holier-than-thou messages about the only route to salvation, a fiery language that made the grand inquisitors of the Catholic Church look comparatively meek. I argued, but of course there is no winning the battle of righteousness among the Christian right.

For a long time I wondered how my southern Italian mother could find a comfortable place for her faith in evangelical Protestantism, and I have come up with only a partial answer to a very complicated process. I think she found a contemporary form of worship that contained elements of ancestral mysticism, but whose medium was modern and accessible: the television set. The embrace of evangelicalism coincided with her increasing anguish over Henry's intractable problems, his inability to hold a job, his inner demons. These men with their fire-and-brimstone fury gave vent to her own. Evangelicalism also provided for my mother, as *Godspell* had done for me, a means to skirt the Church's wish that only priests were authorized to interpret the Bible: she received the blessing to devote herself daily to Scripture.

Prayer cloths, speaking in tongues, anointed waters—my mother sought all of these vehicles because she could not prevent a birth defect, and hoped that a devout faith could heal her son's mental disabilities, seizures, and rage, that a relentless faith could make her offspring whole. Like the Italian women before her who raised fleshy arms and stretched palms to the heavens, tacking tiny silver ex-votos of hearts and legs and heads on saints in search of cures for ailments, my mother found a similar language in evangelicalism as she held with maternal devotion a prayer cloth to her son's forehead.

Her heroes were faith healers, especially a small man named Morris Cerullo, a converted Jew turned evangelical who could tell the Truth in black and white, simple letters, and promise miracles with a wave of his palms. She would attend meetings in large arenas with relatives or friends and come back dazzled by Cerullo's gravelly voice and message of redemption. Ultimately, however, my mother did not abandon Catholicism for this deeply conservative brand of Protestantism; over time her interest faded, perhaps because she grew disillusioned by the lack of change in her life circumstances. The bellowing fervor of that period ended with a mild pitter-patter. These preachers are rarely mentioned today, and she is back to attending weekly mass, now Sunday mornings at 8:00, on time.

While my mother moved away from evangelicalism, my brother Henry inherited some of her former zeal, devoting his days to writing messages on a prayer sheet to his hero, Oral Roberts (who takes money to answer prayers composed in a child's scrawl). Anyone who enters my parents' house must be on guard that religion is in the air they breathe, not just symbolically represented in the statues of saints lining the bedroom dressers. When Henry first met my husband, he asked in an inquisitive interview of his brother-in-law if he ever spoke in tongues, a question as natural to Henry as "What's your line of work?" After receiving a negative answer, he demonstrated in a stream of babble his process of speaking in tongues.

I also share an enthusiasm for heroes of faith, but mine are cerebral, irreverent, and speak in a language I can understand.

Like my mother, I have gone through different phases. In the eighties, I was intrigued by Dorothy Day, whose turbulent youth seemed a textbook example of how *not* to be Catholic, yet who ultimately devoted her life to helping the poor through the Catholic Worker movement, which she founded, and who today is a candidate for sainthood. I spent much of my time as a journalist writing about the homeless and observing people with a social commitment greater than my own create decent living quarters for the poor and mentally ill.

My faith is intimately tied to my sadness over Henry's disability, to the struggle of the lost sheep in a heartless world (I am more comfortable thinking about Henry's illness in terms of his quiet loss, not his turbulent anger). I am drawn to the passages on social justice in Isaiah and the Gospel writings about a fairer scheme of things. Yet each time I see a child who walks in the shadows of the strong, the pretty girl in the toddler playground who looks about eight and hobbles to a horse on a spring, her mother a protective arm's length away, I wonder if the Gospel's promise to bring forth righteousness means anything in her life, or my brother's, or are a solace for my guilt.

I have come to realize that not one Church but many churches stand, and that within this larger community I may seek a comfortable place. My fondness for Jesuits and their intellectual pursuit of matters of faith (which began when I was an undergraduate at Georgetown) has led me more recently to a dark Italian baroque church I occasionally attend that includes questioning Catholics, gays, and lesbians, cardinal deviants all thrown together. There I have met a gifted Jesuit, one of those soldiers of God who finds room between Church canons and his parishioners' needs to bend the rules slightly, and who offers a vision of goodness and abundance, not a weekly reminder of sacrifice and suffering. There I have put aside my lifelong nervousness during mass and can ponder my vision of the Church—that is, a community of people acknowledging to one another the varied ways in which they have taken the tremendous and courageous step toward faith, and not marking an attendance tally sheet, a score card for goodness.

And there I asked this Jesuit to baptize my son. In a private ceremony that was as inclusive as a Catholic sacrament could be, we added a Jewish blessing and made statements about our hopes for our fifteen-month-old (this not-easy decision took months of discussion between my husband and me) which contained quotes from Isaac Bashevis Singer and James Joyce. The ceremony included my brother Bob and a handful of Catholic and Jewish friends, who all gathered in a plain parish office to look over the biblical readings my husband and I had chosen before entering the adjacent church. As the door opened that separated the offices from this immense church, we haltingly entered, the veil of darkness inside partially lifted by rays of a dappled sun, several dim bulbs, and two large white candles resting in tall gold holders. We marveled at the vaulted ceilings and sublime architecture that we had to ourselves for thirty minutes, and absorbed the power of ritual images, the flickering light, flowing water, and scent of musky oil.

I am heartened and saddened by the uniqueness of this church, knowing that within the structure of the Catholic hierarchy such places can exist, but aware that I have found no other like it. Which means that I am often angry with the institutional Church and wonder if I can include myself and child within it: I read about conservative papal decrees, child-abusing priests, the easy availability of celebrity annulments, anti-Semitism during World War II (I've tried to let go of the Inquisition, not wanting to hold a grudge past five hundred years); or, more mundanely, I listen to fearful Catholic high school girls with visions of purgatory in their heads repeat their teacher's admonition: if they don't go to weekly confession before receiving communion, they're committing a serious sin. During these times, I try to take a breath and think about an incident that occurred nearly two decades ago.

I had just graduated from college and was visiting St. Peter's Church in Rome with my brother. Observing Michelangelo's *Pietà*, I became overwhelmed by the sculpture's simple elegance in the midst of the ornate Roman basilica, by the contrast between power and art, papal authority and a mother's grace. A flooding sensation of warmth interrupted my gaze, so powerful that I felt my blood drain and I broke into tears. For the rest of that morning I sensed a new kinship between myself and the strangers who strolled through the basilica, one that ended a few hours later and never took place again. Over the years, I have tried to dismiss the frightening novelty of this moment, yet still want to claim its calm and peace, to see again the shimmer of light in the artist's creation that opens a place for faith.

AS A WOMAN FROM southern Italian stock, I was expected to be devout; my mother would have none of the leeway given to men in the family with their nine-out-of-ten commandments. It took her years to meet her Jewish son-in-law, whom she now gets along with quite well. Her ban on my wedding had as much to do with a deep fear of Henry's reaction to my marriage, a first-time event in our family, as it did with religion. My parents remain afraid of Henry's volatile temper, so the concept of change in the family structure is usually beyond our imagination. And today Henry is jealous, lashing out that I am married and he is not, yet he can still enjoy the company of a man with whom he is comfortable enough to demonstrate speaking in tongues.

Despite my mother's insistence later in life on following a

strict interpretation of Catholic rules, it was her mixing and merging of religious practices when I was growing up that helped shape my view that one's faith is a changing, creative process. In our household, southern Italian Catholicism bowed to a more rigid Irish-American Church, distrustful of folksy irreverence and an array of saints; then the saints came marching in as we waited for roses to drop from the heavens; and just when I least expected it, Protestant Pentecostalism flew through the window with the plucky assurance of a bright-feathered parrot rattling holy jargon.

Through the years, my grandmother's religious articles have been worshiped, tucked away, and embraced again. As I think about the women in my family who have humbled themselves, reddened knees and clasped fists before old wooden dressers, rhythmically chanting to a lambent flame, and who despite a life-time of disappointments return to the well-worn page of a Scripture as if approaching it for the first time; and as I watch old women in Italian-American parishes call upon their mystical roots, pinning ex-votos to life-size statues, making a miles-long pilgrimage for the Virgin Mary, asking her to pay heed to their problems, wearing faith like a comfortable old housedress, I know fondly that I have been shaped by a culture that allows a poet to call some saints scoundrels, but that needs its baroque pageantry of martyred heroes to carry the hopes and prayers of their people, sisters and brothers in search of mercy.

To study the faces of those saints, to find the image of the God of my ancestors in their melancholy countenance, I would venture to describe a loving but imperfect God, whose heaven is as easy or as difficult to comprehend as the deeply flawed earth. One who created so much wine from water that the barrels flowed uninterrupted, flooding the basement; who finds the adulterer a place at heaven's gate and laughs along with the funeral jester. One who sweeps a quarter hour off Sunday mass; who needs an interpreter for the babble of tongues and spends long days at casting calls for an off-Broadway play. One who knows that his people had to weave the knowledge of life and death into the rise and fall of each day.

Work

I tell you, doing things you can touch with your hands
has an advantage: you can make comparisons and
understand how much you're worth. You make a
mistake, you correct it, and next time you don't make it.

—THE CHARACTER LIBERTINI FAUSSONE
IN PRIMO LEVI'S *The Monkey's Wrench*

M Y GRANDFATHER'S WORTH WAS judged by the
strength of his arms, the sharpness of his pickax, the height of
the stone pile smashed at the end of the day, the smoothness of
the tarry black pavement he laid. His years were measured by
heavy rhythms: the pickax, suspended like a brick in the air, then
thrust in the ground; the shush of the shovel that lifted the earth,
the scratch of its blade scooping up gravel. My grandfather respected his projects' foundation, and he would pay the ground
homage, finding time to tend to his beloved vegetable and flower
gardens. He put in a hard day's work; he put his heart into his

work. That was the message I learned from my mother's side of the family: the words "work" and "heart" were inextricably linked.

My maternal grandfather came from the village of Conza della Campania in southern Italy, whose motto was *Lavoro e libertà*, Work and liberty. Yet in Conza neither could be found. The inhospitable climate and rugged terrain made farming an unproductive trade, and the small plots of arable land were mostly the property of middle- and upper-class landowners, keeping the poor poor. My grandfather awoke before sunrise each day and left a small stone shack, whose only luxury was a washbasin, to labor in the fields until the sun turned in. By his early twenties he had had enough of the slavish hours and pitiable compensation, and left Conza for America. In his new country my grandfather's luck would change; after working for a year as a manual laborer, he formed his own business, the Conti Construction Company, which still exists today.

Natale Conte became Tony Conti in the United States, his last name changed by document handlers who couldn't pronounce the Italian *e*, and his first by fellow workers who didn't know an Italian Christmas but had heard of Tonys in construction. "Honest Tony" he was called, the short, stocky Italian laborer who wore a frayed, stain-spotted fedora, white shirt, vest, and thin tie pulled down slightly at the collar. He landscaped, paved driveways, and put in waterlines for the wealthy residents of Short Hills, which probably influenced my mother's choice of this suburb, where she raised her own family. Because my grandfather's work was seasonal, during the winter he would wrap his legs in burlap sacks and walk several miles in the snow to shovel coal at the homes of his customers, who sometimes attached a dollar bill to the tool's wooden handle as a Christmas gift.

Natale died almost fifteen years before I was born, but in pictures I have seen his strong, self-possessed face with a pronounced

nose and square jaw, thick head of black hair (gray in later pho-
tos) perfectly combed back, and faint smile. His vigorous look
was deceptive; his heart succumbed to the daily stress of physical labor, and Natale lived only to the age of sixty.

My grandfather and his two sons, Mickey and George, had
bad hearts; each fought and finally succumbed to that most
metaphoric disease. Perhaps that's why so many stories center on
these men and their endeavors, in which the thick of emotion
overwhelmed rational action. What would the family's history in
construction have been like without my Uncle George's famous
temper, which led to the "1 percent fight"? When my grandfather
died, my uncles took over the firm but they disagreed about how
to form a partnership. My Uncle George, a spirited man, larger-
than-life in both his exploits and his desires, had a stubborn
streak as intense as his blue eyes and jet black hair. George decided
that he deserved 51 percent of the profits because he alone had
been running the company. That left 49 to his older brother
Mickey, who of course disputed the math, and went off on his
own—a family rupture that never was fully repaired. My Uncle
Mickey, whose true love was playing music, didn't have the heart
for construction, and he died young, at forty-eight.

As Conti Construction grew, so did Uncle George's woes. He
left town for long weekends, paid less attention to the company's
bookkeeping, and relegated much of the decision making to an
irresponsible engineer who bid too low on the largest project
that Conti Construction had ever been awarded. The dry land
they were hired to excavate turned out to be a giant swamp, but
Uncle George refused to back away. When George's son, Nat,
spotted an old water main in the ground, the corroded pipes yet
another stumbling block to an already huge miscalculation, Nat
suggested that they subcontract parts of the job.

"I was awarded this contract," Uncle George shouted back

with his usual bluster. "If you don't like it, get your friggin' ass off the job."

Uncle George was determined to transform this swampland into a park. But as they were placing the last pipes in the ground, the old water main blew, the volcanic force of water and cascading sand trapping two men working inside a ditch. In a frantic attempt to escape, one man piggybacked the other—the position in which Nat found their lifeless bodies several hours later, the time it took to dig them out.

George finished the work, but during the long months of this job two men died and he used up Conti Construction's last dollars on a project whose losses were bigger than the company's coffers. He was forced to declare bankruptcy, suffering a crippling personal and business disaster from which he never fully recovered. Yet despite his troubles, plus a series of illnesses that left only half of his heart functioning, throughout his life Uncle George possessed a contagious enthusiasm for the unturned page, embarking on a variety of self-started projects.

As he colored in his landscape of dreams, George's palette modestly ranged from loamy brown to tomato red. He talked for many years about building a restaurant called the Leaning Tower of Pizza. Bad luck followed again when my uncle discovered, driving along a strip of endless highway and neon-lit restaurants, that someone else shared his idea: on the billboard, the fantastical pizza parlor of Uncle George's entrepreneurial visions was already a reality, though slanted from the perpendicular. Eventually he owned the Pizza Mia, a spot for a decent slice, but not quite the Pisa Mia of his imagination.

A few years after George's business had been dissolved, his son Nat, who was taught how to use a short-handed shovel by his father (long-handed shovels are for the lazy because they keep workers too far from the earth), and how to pave driveways and carve animals from stone by his grandfather, started his own Conti Construction Company. Over the years, Nat realized Uncle George's goal; he built a company that today does $100 million of business and employs over six hundred workers. My uncle, never giving up the labor that he loved, worked for Nat, reversing the power structure of their ever-volatile father-son relationship. From the time that I knew Uncle George, he always seemed a step behind his partially fulfilled desire of owning and running Conti Construction.

Uncle George's low voice sounded especially raspy, like that of a jazz musician introducing accompanists mid smoky set, when he spoke to my mother. "Sister," he'd say, "you don't know how hard I work," and he would wipe his brow while my mother served George's requested dish of hot peppers, *tatalles*, and a cold glass of red Gallo wine. She briefly objected to the peppers as bad for his health—the dialogue part of their usual banter—but she always took pleasure in watching her brother voraciously eat what was put before him. Uncle George once explained that doctors had described the shape of his stomach as "prehistoric," which he believed allowed him to digest hot, spicy food despite his bad heart. My uncle's incredible will to live amazed me, and he lived hard, marrying several times (which I only understood through the frequent introduction of new aunts) and, in his words, working "like a dog." I watched his broad face drip with sweat as he poured concrete or carefully unloaded a truck filled with bricks in front of our house; his gaze was careful, concentrated, but also revealed the strenuous pain of physical labor, and no one else I knew brought both body and spirit into each working moment as did Uncle George.

The trade of construction, the pride of my mother's side, would defeat my own family. My father valued education and its path to good-paying jobs, but he also realized that he was a failure at manual labor. Early in my father's working days, he abruptly left the bank that had employed him, and decided that same afternoon to join Conti Construction until he found another job. He made arrangements to begin his new trade with my grandfather, and was sent to work on a job with Uncle George. During World War II, my father was one of the soldiers who built the Alaskan Highway, and he was stationed in Europe throughout the bombings, yet he couldn't keep up with my uncle's demands and schedule. After several weeks of hauling rocks in wheelbarrows, never fast or expert enough, he gave up construction for good. If my father imagined a workday with natural cycles and breaks, or even a moment to sip hot coffee, such a notion was incompatible with George's determination to get the job done.

My brother Bob proved as ineffectual as his father in mastering the Conti skill. Uncle George once came to build new steps in front of our house, replacing a pedestrian chipped red brick with handsome off-white stones and a decorative slate cleaved into the top step. My brother wanted to help, and inquisitively watched my uncle work. But when he was told to stir the cement, his movements were as slow and glutinous as the heavy mixture. He lifted the gooey cement as if playing with an overcooked batch of farina, and slopped it back and forth, forward and backward, using a shovel as his spoon. Entranced by the rhythm, he was startled by a shout: "What the hell are you doing?" My uncle had a temper to match his generous heart. George laid each slab of stone himself and refused to take money for his work; he just wasn't going to coddle my brother, still a young boy with a child's attitude toward work.

My brother, methodical in temperament like my father, was too slow to keep up with the rigors of manual labor, so it was lucky that he decided to become a lawyer. But he, too, had a pas-

sion for working with his hands, and his favorite class throughout junior high and high school was wood shop. He brought
home samples of wood and taught me their names as we savored
the feel, running our fingers along the grain and sniffing the fra-
grant red cedar. His handiwork would become Christmas gifts: a
simple oak desk for me, an end table for our living room, a wal-
nut salad bowl. In high school my brother must have sensed that
there was little room in life for men who used their hands, and he
adjusted his expectations, retiring his tool box as soon as he graduated. While he had not the skill of the fine craftsman, he also
understood that our society values finished products, not the
painstaking process of creating them.

My uncle worked up until his death at the age of seventy-five,
and his labor is planted firmly in the soil, paying him tribute
each day. While the blue-gray and scarlet slate that I placed my
feet on as a little girl has faded, and the white-colored tablets are
now a mossy green, my uncle's steps and walkway are a small
monument to us, his good nature and irascible temper bound
together in the trail of mortar and ferruginous stairway that lead
to my parents' house.

In several of his books and essays, Primo Levi wrote with
great affection about men who worked with their hands, and he
is the most articulate observer to have celebrated the trade of
construction. Levi understood that the careful method of laying
bricks, a process that is corrected, adjusted, guided by a steady
hand, sometimes abandoned, requires a similar attention to detail
as the process of building words on a page. And the belief that,
at the end of the job, a respectable, lasting product will appear demands a leap of faith shared by kindred souls. As an Italian Jew
from Turin, Levi pondered the difference between his Talmudic
heritage, which stressed the life of the mind, and the long history

of skilled artisans in the land where his family had settled. Levi sensed that there was a loss of the self if both parts weren't explored in life. In his memoir *The Periodic Table*, he wrote:

> What were we able to do with our hands? Nothing, or almost nothing. The women, yes—our mothers and grandmothers had lively, agile hands, they knew how to sew and cook, some even played the piano, painted with watercolors, embroidered, braided their hair. But we, and our fathers? Our hands were at once coarse and weak, regressive, insensitive: the least trained part of our bodies. Having gone through the first fundamental experiences of play, they had learned to write, and that was all. . . . [B]ut they were unfamiliar with the solemn, balanced weight of the hammer, the concentrated power of a blade, too cautiously forbidden us, the wise texture of wood, the similar and diverse pliability of iron, lead, and copper. If a man is a maker, we were not men: we knew this and suffered from it.

Levi, a chemist by training and concentration camp survivor who devoted the latter part of his life to writing, was intrigued by masons, coppersmiths, riggers, all men who took pride in manual labor and the tangible results of their work. And he realized that the love of one's work often blooms among those who don't heed a boss's demands and have the freedom to create, from start to finish, something they can call their own.

Considering the strong similarities between the construction worker and the writer, who both faithfully believe in the usefulness of their craft, recognize the self in their creations, respect the freedom these jobs offer, and feel the loneliness of producing a gigantic failure or a small success, Levi notes in his novel *The*

Monkey's Wrench that the failures are a lot more dangerous in construction, and the fatigue certainly isn't the same. Those who
contemplate the moment instead of tackling it don't tire "along
the spine, but higher up; it doesn't come at the end of a weari-
some day, but when you've been trying to make sense of something and have failed. As a rule, sleep doesn't cure it."

In my family, whose ancestors signed their names on documents with an "X," there was no place for books or spare hours
of reflection; man had to be a maker to survive. These men understood that they were alive by the sharp ache along the spine,
welcomed the brief respite of the teasing night only to repeat the
rigors the next morning, and accepted the lifelong pain that men
had died under their watch. They embraced their work but knew
that later generations would seek to abandon manual labor, giving up the satisfaction of making a finished product to pursue the
vague security of becoming middle-class.

I watched my dad go to work in a suit and tie, not a gray shirt
with "Conti Construction" embroidered on its back, and I was
proud of his creased dark trousers that brushed the tongue of his
shiny black shoes. I even used the term "white-collar" to describe
his job, a label that sounded much cleaner and crisper than that
ring of blue around the collar. The certificate my father was
awarded in international commerce from Rutgers University,
where he earned the top scores in his small class, meant that our
family had taken a step toward uncharted territory, the pursuit of
higher education.

In some ways, however, a piece of paper as vague as this certificate clouded for me the meaning of work. I understood construction, but what did my father do as a "traffic manager" for the
Allied Chemical Corporation? For years, when school friends
asked about his work, I had to explain that he wasn't the cop at
the intersection. I still can only vaguely define my father's job,

from which he retired years ago, as having had something to do with the exportation of goods overseas. As a child, all I knew was that he left before I awoke, came home around six-thirty, and often had long business lunches (luncheon dates we called them), which meant he'd snack on a sandwich when we ate a hot dinner. But how many office jobs, filled with endless meetings and memos, deliver something permanent at the end of the day?

Levi was also making a political point, attempting to find a common language to express the collective desires of blue-collar workers and intellectuals. He was writing about the social conditions in Italy, where among the upper classes labor was considered base and the absence of a need to work commanded respect. But in this country the sentiment is the same; we place little value on manual labor, lumping ethnics together by trade and class. I have seen young Italian-American men leave construction to take desk jobs, giving up the freedom found in the slow stroke of the paintbrush, along the curve of a molding chiseled to its nineteenth-century form, or behind the wheel of a bulldozer on an expanse of country brush. They're not earning more money, are frustrated by the long hours and low wages, but hope to gain the prestige that supposedly accompanies wearing a shirt and tie. An acquaintance of mine, after landing and leaving a series of jobs selling computers, told me how his most recent computer job had the potential to be creative—"like contracting was for me." I wondered why he hadn't stayed in contracting, the job he had held when I first met him and admired his work, but remembered that his wife had encouraged him to leave the trade.

The educated Italian-American workforce prides itself on its success in escaping the earlier fate of a lifetime in construction, and many have transcended their working-class roots by entering law and business, occupations that have established a reputable place in society. But at what cost have we forsaken the pleasure, intimacy, and skill of using the hands and heart, of expressing a part of the self in one's work?

The importance of craft was replaced long ago by assembly work, quick production, and the desire to earn a profit. I can only imagine the pleasure my grandfather experienced in his work until his death, and I believe that Uncle George, despite his misfortunes, never felt more alive than when on a construction site. "Son," he'd say—he often addressed family members with the generic noun—"I want to work till the end and die fast." When George was in his mid-seventies with poor hearing and a failing heart, his son worried about the dangers to his father of working on a construction site. Nat decided to put George behind a desk, placing him in charge of company purchasing.

"It was like taking a wild animal out of the field," Nat recalled. Eventually company workers had to build George a soundproof office to control the volume of his daylong cursing. Perhaps his frustration grew with the knowledge that years before, he had stepped onto an empty landscape and, within a certain amount of time, an object, sometimes beautiful, had emerged; as the job was completed, the magic of transformation disappeared and a new project was taken on, the titillation found in the continuing process, not the fixed ending. My grandfather and uncle sought perfection in their shared trade—they would not allow a ripple of cement on a sidewalk; they cut patches of grass with a knife before digging the earth to install waterlines; they made sure that every corner was perfectly tooled, every job built to code. Both men understood few greater joys than the precision of a solid foundation, a centered level, the correct mix of mortar.

IF MY UNCLE GEORGE never achieved the glory he sought and demanded from life, he may have found it in death. George once remarked that he had spent so much time turning over dirt that he didn't want to be buried in it. Before my uncle died in 1991, he asked to be cremated.

Like most passionate, boundary-breaking men who live to fulfill the immigrant dream, Uncle George had extreme desires. He often talked about the luck of the astronaut who could touch the moon's deep craters, explore the infinite wonder of the cosmos, travel far, far from the heavy earth that he shoveled. Several years before he died, Uncle George began to correspond with a company that was proposing to launch a person's ashes into outer space. For Uncle George, heart and work were bound in a combustible mixture; the man whose fiery presence on a construction site jolted workers out of their complacency wanted his ashes blasted from a rocket canister that would soar into the brilliance of the galaxies. By the time of his death, the idea still hadn't gotten off the ground, but his children remembered their father's wish, and when the company announced this one-of-a-kind flight, they made sure that George's remains would be on board.

In the spring of 1997, Uncle George joined Timothy Leary and "Star Trek" creator Gene Roddenberry for what the media dubbed "the first space funeral." A front page *New York Times* article stated: "In a new episode in space travel, not to mention the funeral business, a rocket carrying capsules of [Leary's] ashes and those of 23 others was launched from a plane after takeoff from Grand Canary Island off the Moroccan coast." Also included on this journey, the story continued, were "a space physicist, scientists and pilots," whose powdery remains were supposed to orbit "every ninety minutes for two years, perhaps as many as ten." The reporter didn't mention Uncle George, our family's first space pioneer of sorts, or the fact that Uncle George's ashes were launched for free (the private Houston company charged five thousand dollars to transport each vial, the size of a lipstick container) because he was the first person to have corresponded with the company.

My family gathered together to watch news reports of the American *Pegasus* rocket blasting into space with Uncle George's ashes, a triumphal lifting of his entrepreneurial visions into another sphere. If a lifetime of shoveling stone meant that George had spent his days staring at Medusa's legacy, even her heavy gaze must have dissolved upon his death, as his remains were swept upward by the winged Pegasus that sprang from the Gorgon's body, soaring, weightless in the transcendence of a job well done.

Ancestors

ADEEP BLUE SKY furtively peeked through the clouds on the chilly October morning that I roamed the battered terrain of Conza della Campania to find the remains of my grandfather Natale's house. Wandering the old southern Italian city felt like a stroll in an unkept Roman forum: tall grass, bramble, and the ruins and rubble from an earthquake that shook the region two decades ago covered the ground. Conza has perpetually struggled against the forces of nature since 990, when the town, then under Norman rule, suffered its first recorded earthquake. Parts of Conza (which over the centuries was variously named Compsa, Consa, Cossa, and Cosa) suffered significant earthquake damage in 1349, 1466, 1694, 1732, 1737, and in 1980, when, at the epicenter of an earthquake that devastated the south, the entire village was destroyed in ninety seconds and more than 10 percent of the population was killed.

My husband and I, accompanied by Conza's former Mayor Raffaele Farese and my third cousin Franco, saw what had passed for places to live, narrow stucco hovels, one next to the other, occasionally adorned with a wrought-iron balcony. Semicircular slabs of stone were cemented to the walls of homes to serve as parking places for donkeys. Farese's knowledge of Conza, where he presided as mayor for twenty years, was formidable, and he walked through the rubble slightly hunched, his face impermeably sad. His chiseled, dignified features were the shadow of a once proud visage; in the same cursed year, Farese lost his title of mayor and his beloved town to the earthquake. Farese handed me a booklet about the town, and I was struck by the motto of Conza in black type, *Lavoro e libertà,* Work and freedom, absent of any irony. The peasants began their day before sunrise, working until sunset harvesting corn, wheat, olives, grapes, apples, and pears on a plain whose checkerboard patches of yellow and brown produced meager and inferior food. Because of the poor quality of the soil, even today the cost of harvesting a crop is higher than its retail value.

The earthquake had toppled all but one wall of my grandfather's house; the remaining milky gray stone stood amid the weeds. Stalks of grass blanketed the floor. The house once had a small living room, an upstairs bedroom, wine cellar, and sink; unimaginably, at one point eight people—including my grandfather's brother, his wife, and children—lived side by side in these tiny quarters. The outdoor toilet, added in 1950, now resembled a large potted plant as clusters of green shoots sprouted through the base and dangled over the rim. I snapped a picture to bring back home; when my mother saw it, she let out a cry of disbelief. My grandfather owned the title to the property, but after leaving Italy for America, he had intended for his brother Antonio to inherit it. Antonio was afraid, however, that my mother and her siblings would try to reclaim the home. She couldn't believe that this shack was Antonio's prized possession, which he had spent a lifetime fearing would be taken from him by his brother's children.

FOR MANY YEARS, I was too frightened to travel to the south of Italy. I had read Carlo Levi and Ann Cornelisen's poetic accounts of this heartless land. I pondered the meaning of Levi's now famous title, *Christ Stopped at Eboli*. The peasants said that Christ could not have traveled farther south than the fertile land of Eboli—which is about thirty-five miles north of my paternal grandparent's town, Picerno. "We're not Christians," they told Levi, an Italian Jew from Turin banished in 1935 to the village of Gagliano in Basilicata because of his opposition to Fascism. The peasants meant that they were not "human beings," they were too far below the status of the blessed. "The seasons pass today over the toil of the peasants," wrote Levi, "just as they did three thousand years before Christ; no message, human or divine, has reached this stubborn poverty."

I had also heard family stories that evoked an unimaginably poor place inhabited by primitive people. My cousin Joey, my father's nephew who is now in his seventies and tells tales with the quick wit and rapid-fire speech of a much younger man, lived for several years in southern Italy in the 1970s. He and his wife Concetta, nicknamed Lady because she was the only girl in the family, moved to the *paese* of Lady's relatives. My cousin described a place that missed its passage into the twentieth century; a feudal fortress of landless peasants bound to the gentry. The town had a crier who arrived in the center of the piazza at 8:00 A.M. to shout the news of the day; hired wailers mourned at funerals; the local doctor was equipped only with a dentist's chair. My cousin went to the doctor/dentist's office when Lady's aunt was slipping from the final moments of life.

"Is she dead?" the doctor asked.

"I think so," replied my cousin, "but that's why I came to you."

"If you think she's dead, she's dead," he said, and handed my cousin a death certificate form.

The descriptions of Lady's aunt going about her day called to mind images of typical peasant women: she poked her fingernail in fruit to get a discount from the merchant, yelled at her spendthrift niece because she tossed a squeezed lemon in the garbage, and refused the modern conveniences of a refrigerator and stove that they had bought for her. My cousin, using the necessary setups and pauses of a good teller, affectionately recreated the anachronisms of southern Italian life and offered the kind of intimate knowledge that children of immigrants crave: he verified my parents' inalienable luck in escaping this bleak land. Sometimes his stories were so profoundly sad that their shocking conclusion left me speechless. Poverty overwhelmed the peasants' days, and abuse was a natural part of the life cycle.

Visiting a peasant family they knew who lived on the top floor of a shack, with the animals kept below, my cousins were invited inside by one of the daughters. As they were talking with the young girl, my cousin turned to his wife and asked, "Do you hear a baby crying?"

"It must be the animals," she replied. A little while later, he heard another cry and mentioned it to the girl.

"Oh, my mom had a baby since you were last here," she said matter-of-factly, and pulled from under the bed a whimpering infant tied to a slab of wood. The binding of the infant to the board, once a common practice in southern Italy, was thought to prevent rickets, a disease of the skeletal system actually caused by a lack of exposure to sunlight. The mother had to work in the fields, so she tied up her infant each morning, believing that the ropes and wood were beneficial to the health of her child, and kept the baby under the bed until she could return home.

My cousin's stories were over twenty years old, and the village of Lady's family was much poorer than the town of Conza. But I believed that the south had never changed, and with trepidation I prepared for my trip. Asking my mother even perfunctory questions before leaving proved useful. Because southern Italians usually name their children after a grandparent, parent, or close relative, I discovered the family's tidy symmetry. Natale had four children in America: Michele (Mickey); Gerardo (George or Jerry); Natalia (Natalie); and my mother Concetta (Constance or Connie). Antonio, who never left Conza but remained in close contact with his brother, also named his children Michele, Gerardo, Natalina, and Concetta; and all of Antonio's children except Michele, who died young like my Uncle Mickey, were still alive. Rediscovering this lost half was much easier than I had anticipated. A cousin from New Jersey gave my mother the telephone number of a man she knew who frequently traveled to Conza. This man gave me Raffaele Farese's number. Farese, or *professore*, as we called him, was also the town's former high school English teacher, and he proved to be an invaluable guide, although his English was several decades rusty. Before we left New York, I contacted the *professore*, who told my mother's first cousin Concetta of our arrival, and they arranged for her nephew Franco to meet us at the Jolly Hotel in Avellino.

Franco, my gregarious cousin and the village electrician, was close to me in age, and so unlike the fatalistic peasants I had encountered in southern Italian literature. Our animated tour guide was above average height and carried a paunch with pride, proof of his robust appetite for food and life. He arrived with his wife Lucia, and they quickly whisked us into the car to begin the hour-and-a-half journey to my grandparents' village. Like all of my cousins in Conza, Franco couldn't speak English. The car ride initiated my long week of language performance which began with a poor textbook Italian and soon degenerated into pantomime and pictures. Just when I thought I had a clue as to what Franco was saying, he would become excited and quicken the pace of his speech, mixing Italian with southern dialect. Lucia would try to intercede, speaking slowly, allowing me time to clear my hazy head, aching from the sudden immersion in the clipped syllables and idioms of the south. It would take me a few days to understand Franco.

En route to Conza, Franco proudly pointed out sights of interest, like the village where former Italian prime minister Ciriaco De Mita grew up (I thought about my Roman friends snickering at De Mita's speeches filled with "incomprehensible" dialect). Franco told me about his aunts and uncles now in their sixties and seventies, and I discovered that Antonio had two more daughters: Teresa, Franco's mother; and Giuseppina, who had immigrated to Australia years ago. I also learned that Franco and his forty-four-year-old sister Maria were the only two grandchildren of Antonio left in Conza; all the others had moved to the outskirts of Milan, Switzerland, and Australia, and were employed mainly as waiters or factory workers.

Antonio's six children, my mother later told me, were the centerpiece of the brothers' cross-Atlantic correspondence—and rivalry. While Antonio was proud of the older Natale, like most siblings he was also competitive and regretted the lost opportunity to get his children out of southern Italy. In the letters Antonio sent to his brother, he belittled Natale's achievements in America, writing that he was the one truly blessed, with a larger family in Conza.

Franco drove us to where we would be staying, the home of Antonio's daughter, my mother's first cousin Concetta, nicknamed Concettina because of her tiny size. Concettina, a squat and sturdy woman with warm brown eyes and a pleasant round face, was in her early seventies and dressed in black like most

Italian women her age, mourning the death of her husband, who had suffered a heart attack the year before. Her diminutive stature and dove gray and white hair cut in short spikes made her resemble, my husband thought, a southern Italian Gertrude Stein; and Concettina was similarly "as sturdy as a turnip," in the words of essayist Elizabeth Hardwick.

Concettina greeted me with a tight embrace, and I towered over her, as I do when hugging my own mother, standing more than half a foot taller and feeling the awkwardness of the disparity in size. She clutched my hand tightly and then released it to wipe away her tears. Concettina dried her watery eyes by moving the back of her hand in a brisk semicircular motion over her closed lids, like a baby prying away sleepiness. Her eyes filled frequently with tears, and Concettina's instinct to comfort herself with the hard back of her hands, rather than callused fingertips permanently darkened by planting and harvesting, suggested that she had tilled the soil for many years.

I had prepared myself and my husband for a stay in a tiny shack, but her home was lovely, larger than the one I grew up in. Today's Conza is a bit of an anomaly in southern Italy. Throughout the eighties, its residents, displaced by the earthquake, doubled up with family or lived in temporary trailer housing until the government sent plows to build new homes on fallow land that is now called Nuova Conza. Concettina's home was paid for by the central Italian government's earthquake relief fund, and her family added some of their own money for construction because their house cost more than the allocated government subsidy. Concettina's husband and sons used their Italian artistry to build a simple two-story white stucco home with a curved wrought-iron balcony that wrapped around the second floor and a terracotta shingled roof. Inside, a smooth marble banister led to the home's empty top floor, which was intended for her son and his family, who now live in Milan; the space included two bedrooms, a bathroom, and a fully equipped kitchen. Concettina lived alone on the first floor of her large house, and spent most of her time in the white tiled kitchen with fireplace before retiring to the adjacent bedroom.

I was delighted to see this gift of new homes to residents who had suffered a decade of displacement. But I am also used to the American response to natural calamities, not this unfamiliar form of government justice. Our disaster victims don't get free new homes, only much ballyhooed federal low-interest loans. I quickly tried to bury an echo of the old sibling competition. It's easier to lament poverty, to follow the long tradition of outsiders going to southern Italy equipped with compassion and its insidious companion, superiority, than to accept that Concettina's pretty, large house with its gated white and pink brick entranceway didn't match my version of the American immigrant story. I was ashamed of my embarrassment that my parents had so little to show for generations of hard work.

After spending just a day with Concettina, however, Nuova Conza reminded me of a Potemkin village. Most of the residents can't afford to pay for electricity to heat these large, poorly insulated homes, and by the time of our late October visit, a deep chill had already set in. While I once blamed my sensitivity to the cold on my Mediterranean ancestry, this illusion quickly burst. A thick bed of clouds streaked in dull gray announced the arrival of the long winter season, and, like a schoolyard bully who wouldn't disappear, taunted us throughout our stay. Inside Concettina's house, the temperature dipped to about forty-six degrees Fahrenheit, and the space heater she dug up kept blowing a fuse. I was eight weeks pregnant, nauseated and freezing, piling layer upon layer of clothing each night in the hope of getting some sleep.

Franco, the electrician, tried to help with the blown fuse, but there was little he could do. He told us not to use the space heater if we turned on the hot-water tank, which took several hours to heat. Every morning my husband and I alternately performed a desperate act of climbing out of the blankets, running to the bathroom to flip on the water-tank switch, sprinting back to the covers, waiting, shutting off the tank to turn on the heater, and finally dipping ourselves in water before dressing. Most of the time the space heater blew a fuse within minutes and the water was ice-cold, yet we couldn't abandon the ritual of our morning ablutions. The only form of heat was Concettina's kitchen fireplace, and before bedtime we would sit for half an hour next to the luxurious flames, trying not to think about the long cold night ahead upstairs.

Franco explained that the cost of electricity to heat Concettina's home almost equaled her monthly pension. Concettina, however, used to a lifetime without central heating, had no complaints about her living quarters, which were lush and beautiful compared to the dilapidated homes of her siblings Natalina and Teresa, who lived outside Conza. Only Concettina, Gerardo, and their niece Maria had both the bad and good fortune to have their homes destroyed by the earthquake and to be the beneficiaries of the government rescue.

The high-spirited Franco served as the master of ceremonies throughout our trip; he introduced us to each relative, provided details of the family history, and had plenty of time to take us around Conza and its surrounding villages because the electrician in a town that can hardly afford electricity is often out of work. As Franco drove us to neighboring hill towns, we followed a steep, curving passageway back to the Middle Ages. Within the walled villages, women all in black balanced firewood on their heads as they walked, and donkeys were used to transport goods. We were jolted back to modernity only by the television antennas attached to rooftops. Many of the local villagers don't own washing machines, and San Andrea, the largest nearby town, supplies its version of a public Laundromat. Inside the newly renovated "Laundromat," a stream of water was piped along the base of a long, curved, grayish-black stone; ridges were carved into an adjacent slab of stone so women could pound clean large loads of laundry. One of the few public gathering spots for local women (along with the cemetery) the Laundromat was especially festive before weddings, the occasion bringing brides and their mothers together to prepare the trousseau.

WITHIN THE SYMMETRY OF family names, Maria was my counterpart—she is the granddaughter of Antonio; we are both the great-granddaughters of Michele and Concetta Conte. She married her first cousin Donato, Concettina's son who died young, so Maria is both Concettina's niece and her daughter-in-law. Though I look more southern Italian (in the American imagination at least) than Maria, who is fair with light brown hair, it was she who inherited the limited options of the land. She lives with her two teenage daughters in a large Nuova Conza home on her widow's pension, works in the fields, and cleans houses for "good families"—but "only when she wants to," her brother Franco and daughter Anna both told me with protective pride. Franco and Anna spoke most of the time for the quiet and reserved Maria. I regretted my lapses in Italian because without Franco's eagerness to keep talking until we managed to understand each other, Maria and I only shyly exchanged smiles. I wanted to know if the choice to remain in Conza when all the other granddaughters of Antonio had moved away was hers, or if the death of her husband permanently sealed her fate, tying her to the south. Any anger or bitterness may have been tempered by Maria's obvious pride in her large, handsome government-built home. Her pension and small income gave her daughters Concetta and Anna the cherished items of teenage life: a stereo and television set, linking them to American and Italian pop culture. Their bedroom looked like those of most teenagers, with posters of hunky men tacked on the walls; in one corner the girls had stacked dozens of empty soda cans, a tower of Coca-Cola red. Maria's older daughter Concetta was studying to be a secretary, and diligently tapped the keys of an electric typewriter to compose a family tree that I had been writing in longhand. But Franco told me that it would be impossible to find a secretarial job because there are no offices in Conza. Concetta planned to work in the pizzeria in San Andrea upon her graduation from high school.

Maria hosted a dinner party where fourteen of us gathered at the dining room table to eat young Concetta's tasty pizza and a platter of antipasto. The children of Antonio posed for a picture, but only their youngest brother Gerardo, who had driven from his home in Switzerland to meet me, managed to smile. Sitting among them, watching them slowly abandon their stoic postures to enjoy the food and each other's company, I thought about the tag of "amoral familism," this notion that peasants act in their own narrow, selfish interest, helping only family members. The label seemed even more absurd after I visited southern Italy; within the confines of this arduous life with few outside pleasures, family is a resource, a salvation. Extended families are also large, and to feed their many members is in itself an act of generosity. Unlike my mother and her remaining sibling, these sisters and brother, nieces and nephews, see each other constantly. They took great delight in showing me their photo albums, fingering each page with seemingly endless fascination as they described gatherings that defined their years.

In the face of Gerardo, a retiree living on his government pension who spends every summer in Conza, I saw the Conte genes.

Gerardo resembled and reminded me of his namesake in America, my Uncle George. Meeting Gerardo several years after the death of his older cousin brought back memories of George's short and full body, his thick head of hair (and wide sideburns that Uncle George had grown in the seventies), his lack of attention to serious illness, and his relentless enthusiasm. Both men had open-heart surgery, were casual about their medicine, loved to drink wine, and shared a passion for hot peppers. While both spent a lifetime in hard manual labor, their days shaped by the earth they shoveled, Gerardo had taken on a wider variety of trades, including a stint as a chimney sweep in France ("I got all black," he told me).

"Work, there is no work," Franco lamented, and Gerardo nodded in agreement. "I've got to leave here," Franco told us throughout our stay, yet admitted that he had no future plans. Each day these men talked about work; the word became an incantation encapsulating my relatives' lost dreams and foiled plans in Italy and their inability to escape to America.

"I heard about your uncle's construction company," Gerardo told me, referring to my Uncle George. I was surprised because my mother and her siblings had never corresponded with Gerardo—or with any of Antonio's children.

"I used to do construction work. I wanted to come over, but how could I get working papers? I would have had to marry an American." He mused that if only he could have married the daughter of my great-aunt, Natale and Antonio's half sister. . . . My great-aunt had visited Conza many years ago; she must have talked about Conti Construction and left a picture of her daughter. *Una bella donna*, said Gerardo, his voice trailing as we looked at our cousin's picture in a photo album.

In southern Italy, I had unearthed a mirror image of my mother's family, distorted by years of separation and the decision by my grandfather to abandon this brutal life. Natale and Antonio would never see each other again, but the faces of their children, one named after the next, became a reflection on the sea between them. The memory of Concetta Conte, whose last years were spent under the watchful eye of nuns, would be borne by her granddaughters, my mother and Concettina, though my mother was embarrassed by the foreign sound of the name and, like most Italian-American Concettas, changed it to Connie. Despite the acute differences in their surroundings, both my mother and her cousin Concettina, I imagined, could have been close friends if destiny had placed them in the same village. I could easily see them drinking coffee in the morning, homemade wine in the afternoon, talking about the tragedies that have shaped their lives: Concettina's son dying young, my mother having a mentally retarded child, now fifty-three, whom she still cares for. The years have weighed more heavily on Concettina, a solemn woman who looks older and more worn from a lifetime in the fields, than on my mother, who has always veiled her sorrow with laughter and aimless chatter. But both Concettina and Connie, only a few years apart in age, have numbed their sadness through relentless work, which defines and lends a structure to their days. Even on Sundays, Concettina can be found in her small backyard vineyard by 8:00 A.M. picking grapes to sell in front of her home later that day. After a full day of working in her garden, cooking, and cleaning, she sits alone at night weaving white coverlets. The rhythm of the intricate hand-stitching, she told me, has helped her sleep since her husband died.

Every day my mother performs her meticulous housework, cooking and cleaning, washing and ironing each item of clothing. She even presses Hanes underwear. She arranges the day in such a way as to give herself, at the most, a half hour of rest, and rarely leaves the house except to go to the grocery store and weekly mass. While her seasons do not revolve around planting and harvesting, she has her own perennial projects like washing windows and curtains in the fall and spring.

My mother has always passed up objects that could simplify a life that holds no place for leisure. She has never owned a clothes dryer (what could be better than fresh air?), and her children pointlessly talked her into installing a dishwasher, which she only uses on major holidays, after she has washed each plate by hand. Work for both Concettas is a ritual; the exertion and exhaustion associated with it give rise to a sense of accomplishment and contentment, readying each woman for the next morning.

To watch the small acts that composed my relatives' days—the careful preparation of a meal and fastidious cleanup, the whirl of women serving men, the laughter provoked by a nod to our common ancestry, like shared foods and dialect words—the deep chasm that I thought separated my family from this tiny backward village seemed more a surface tear grown wider by the neglect of years. (Or, in the words of my grandmother from Conza, if you don't sew a tiny hole right away, soon you'll be able to stick your whole foot through it.)

My mother's approach to life exists in the shadows of my own, a life that is very different from hers. I have inherited her sense of work's importance, have great difficulty imagining a right to pleasure, and know the security that sorrow holds. Sadness has been tried and tested, inseparable from the scheme of things, while happiness provokes and teases, then leaves us for a better mate. Genetically and culturally, I am a part owner of the past, my temperament shaped by a random fall of chromosomes and the nurturing of my parents. We may think that we are modern creatures, but who isn't linked in some way to tribal rituals, ancient customs? I am carried from one moment in life to the next searching for enough wood to knock on (or, as a child, to run around), always waiting for the next shoe to drop. The legacy of village life doesn't disappear by crossing the ocean; it is transported and adapted, and traces will emerge in the blink of a century's eye.

Each of us constructs an identity, cuts and tailors it to suit our needs. Traveling to southern Italy, collecting impressions, touching the crude rock of my grandfather's house, letting propinquity establish connection, does not make me a southern Italian. But my identity as an Italian-American of southern Italian descent can now be based on actual heritage, not on what I wanted to be, whether an eastern European Jew in high school or northern Italian later in life.

I could say that my family traces its roots to Dante Alighieri, a ridiculous lie. Or I could say that I was at home arriving in Rome because of my Italian roots, which is not an out-and-out lie but a skewed interpretation of facts based on my wants at the time; the terra-cotta landscape, my visceral connection to dark-haired people, the streams of olive oil were more familiar to me than the atmosphere in London, yet Rome is a world away from the poverty and isolation of southern Italy. Or I could argue that some of my personality traits are linked to a peasant ancestry, which again is a stretch of the imagination, another form of gamesmanship. My myths, however, will merge with a basic truth: in this Möbius strip of my mother's ancestry, fate twisted and placed her on the American side, yet the story comes together, and begins, in southern Italy.

THE LONGER I SPENT in Conza, the more I acted like a novice archaeologist excavating family traits from the rubble of an earthquake, observing how lives so incongruous with my own could meet at such unlikely junctures. The rites of the dead helped me understand the difficult transition for the living who were abruptly transplanted to America. With an aging population and no leisure outlet other than the ubiquitous television set, honoring the dead fills a large part of life in Conza. The talk of the day is about the dead and the dying. The center of town activity is the cemetery, which is visited more often than the church, at least twice a week. I had never seen a cemetery filled with so many fresh flowers. The small secluded area housed a mausoleum containing over two hundred coffins stacked in rows, and mixed bouquets of carnations, daisies, roses, freesia, and lilies sat in copper vases welded to the tombstones. Alongside each vase was a mounted black-and-white photograph of the deceased. Not a wilted petal could be seen, and the day's dappled sunlight and soft floral colors brushed the inscriptions and warmed the cool stone. The colors and scents were a luxury only for the dead, a renewal of the living's devotion; the homes I visited were not brightened by freshly cut flowers.

Surrounded by this marble tribute to the souls of Conza, I understood for the first time one of my grandmother's most pressing fears. "Mama always said we wouldn't visit her grave, and she was right," my mother would say, chiding herself and her siblings over the truth of the prophecy. Her parents were buried near a crime-ridden area about forty minutes from where we lived, and as the years went by, my mother visited less and less until she stopped altogether.

"Mama was right," I heard throughout my childhood, words I grew to resent. What was the purpose of my grandmother's complaint, which left my mother with lifelong guilt? I pragmatically wondered what difference the visits would make if no one was available to greet the guests. But spending time in Conza, I understood that my grandmother's lament had its source in the sad realization that she had raised her daughter in a new land with different rules. Day after day, the villagers of Conza tip their hats to each other as they cross the path of the dead; they come to replace the flowers and kneel in memory of their parents, siblings, and children. My grandmother was denied this same honor by her own children; her grave has become overgrown with weeds, sullied through the decades.

During a drive with Franco, we stopped to see some neighbors who lived in a filthy two-room shack; the old wooden floor, with frayed and bent beams, collected dirt from the fields, and dust covered the home's worn furnishings. The house contained few possessions, revealing not the slow accumulation of years of living but the sparseness of decades denied of leisure. Nearing the end of their lunchtime meal, the sallow-faced couple sat hunched at the table with a friend, sucking bones steeped in tomato sauce while several cats and dogs circled for leftovers. The husband and wife treated us as prized guests because their son had moved to Brooklyn, and they assumed that we would have met him in New York. The woman took out a bag of chocolates, a rare delicacy, and kindly offered a piece as her husband found his son's name and address written on the envelope of a letter they had received.

"Is Brooklyn a *paese?*" my cousin Gerardo asked, using the term for a village as he tried to imagine this vague entity. Kind of, I replied, a large *paese.*

They asked a few more questions about Brooklyn, we said our good-byes and apologized that we hadn't met their son. In the car, I asked Franco and Gerardo why the couple didn't live in Nuova Conza, because their shack had suffered some damage from the earthquake. Franco replied that the government had built them a new home, but they were saving it for their son in Brooklyn. They only visit the house on Sundays because during the week they work in the fields and don't want to get it dirty.

The old wooden hovel, by American standards, would have

blended into the squalor of the poorest parts of Appalachia, yet they preferred to keep a brand-new home untouched just in case their son might return to Conza. Franco's explanation seemed absurd until I recognized a germ of behavior that I know well, having grown up in a family of savers. My mother has always tucked away any possession she considers too good to use. For years she kept a damask tablecloth in a box while serving a holiday meal on a torn hand-stitched one. My father will wear a tattered sweater while five new ones, gifts from his children, sit untouched in his drawer. When my brother bought china in England for my parents' fiftieth wedding anniversary, my mother promptly stored the box in the garage, explaining that she plans to pass it along to us. My brother ignored the comment, unpacked the pieces, and put them in the breakfront. She refuses to take them out. As the peasants felt unworthy of their new home, a present from the government, my mother feels unworthy of any gift she receives; her children will be the inheritors of these small glories.

Perhaps I am romanticizing things to imagine that a part of my mother would be more comfortable in a backward village than in a fancy suburb, and to find elements of this behavior in myself so I too may connect, securing a place in a history. No one in my family would consider packing their bags for southern Italy, but we already carry remnants of the land. Keeping a dress I bought two years ago untouched in my closet, still awaiting the perfect occasion, doesn't open the door to my ancestral DNA. But to find a possible source for this action somehow makes the current less overpowering, more navigable. What once seemed purely a punishing behavior, my mother's self-inflicted martyrdom, my controlled carefulness, may have been born in the fields of abject poverty where to dream of luxury was a simpleton's illusion, and to inherit it the stuff of stories. To tuck a possession away keeps it safe, ready for the end of the fairy tale when the peasant becomes the princess.

"IS THIS ABOUT AN imbroglio?" asked the gray-haired woman with several missing teeth who had carefully watched us through the window of her front door before daring to step outside. It was a dreary afternoon in Picerno, a small village that possesses the charm of a Swiss hill town from a distance but, once the majesty of height disappears, is worn and ragged up close. I had been in Picerno only a few hours and already my presence was considered intrusive.

We had left Conza in the morning with Gerardo and Franco, who generously offered to drive us to the town of my father's family. I knew that my father had wanted to visit Picerno when he was stationed in Italy during World War II, but had only traveled as far south as the regional capital of Potenza. The train for Picerno left every other day, and an army officer didn't have the luxury to wait. Over a half century later, I would take on the task of countless granddaughters of immigrants and report to him about the place where his parents and older siblings once lived. My father's family, like many other immigrants, traveled to America twice. My grandfather brought his wife and four children to New Jersey, but he suffered a stomach ailment that the local Italian doctor thought could only be cured by the tinned produce and flavorless meats of southern Italy. They packed their bags and returned to Picerno for several years, but eventually came back to Millburn, where my grandmother gave birth to three more children.

Gerardo knew the map of the country roads by heart and announced every crevice and hole seconds before we bounced in the back of Franco's car. When we reached the new *autostrada*, this once long journey to the northern region of Basilicata took about an hour and a half.

We immediately headed to Picerno's town hall, open a half day on Saturdays, and sought the help of small clerk nicknamed Tonino, who wearing jeans, a pullover sweater, and a day's stubble of a beard seemed anxious to close his office for the weekend until he learned of the presence of two Americans. The old and cluttered *municipio* housed several bookshelves of notebooks containing marriage and death certificates, and Tonino pulled out those from the late 1800s to locate information about my grandparents. Unfortunately for us, the town hall clerk spent more time making calls to find out about a relative in the States than looking for our family records. In the small world of southern Italian immigrants, we discovered that his relative lived ten minutes from my parents.

"Is he from Summit?" I asked.

"No, no. Soom-eat," Tonino replied several times.

Distracted by leafing through the notebooks, at least twenty minutes passed before I realized that we were describing the same town. Ultimately, we found only one piece of paper relating to my family, the death certificate of my great-grandmother that included her address. We left his office to search the narrow streets for her home.

After lunch, of course. The prospect of discovering the past had to wait; Gerardo and Franco needed spaghetti and wine to replenish them after the long drive. Gerardo and Franco, uncle and nephew, wore green and plum knit shirts pulled tightly over ample bellies and made an amusing detective team, the Starsky and Hutch of southern Italy. They relayed far too much information to everyone we met, kicking off the search for my father's family by explaining how they were related to my mother's side. They enthusiastically spoke to all within earshot, beginning with the toothless restaurant cook who didn't know of the Laurinos but left a steaming pot of water behind as she set out to find her ninety-year-old neighbor, the village historian. A few minutes later, she reappeared with a dignified man wearing a sport jacket, wool vest, and checked shirt buttoned to the collar. He had no memory of my family but kindly posed for a picture; his reserved demeanor and piercing blue-green eyes reminded me of my father and his oldest brother, and with no proof of the Laurino presence in Picerno, I settled for this meager contribution to my photo album.

The town of Picerno, with a faded piazza that housed a tobacco and dressmaker's shop, was larger and more urban than Conza. After lunch we roamed its circuitous cobbled roads and eventually stumbled upon the street listed on the death certificate. But an attractive modern house brightened by an orange shingled roof stood where my great-grandmother had supposedly lived. The old woman who had been staring at us from the inside foyer cautiously opened the door. She wore a dark crocheted shawl over a cotton housedress, white anklets, and slippers, the cold wind slapping her bare legs.

There was no imbroglio, Franco repeated several times. I was not an unwelcome intruder but an American searching for a piece of her past. We must have looked sympathetic because the woman's face eventually softened, and she found a friend who took us around another winding path. I'm not sure what both women were looking for, but we walked for a while until they abruptly stopped to tell us that they couldn't help, they knew of no Laurinos. In Picerno my story would have no neat endings, or beginnings; I would discover no relatives or grandparents' homes.

Only the dead revealed the past. In the Picerno cemetery, which sat at the bottom of the hill, we found the grave of my great-grandmother, and I saw our family name inscribed on several tombstones. I cried at my great-grandmother's grave and was embarrassed by this flood of tears for a woman I knew nothing about. I cried, I believe, for memories never granted.

During our journey back, we stopped at Eboli. The fields were a deep green, so different from the prickly brown that covers Conza and Picerno. Eboli's ability to produce a real harvest has meant that its people can shop in clothes stores and drink in espresso bars, and buy gifts, luxuries that were foreign to my relatives. I went into a store and quickly purchased a token of thanks for Concettina, Gerardo, and Franco: a silver picture frame, a ceramic bowl, and a bud vase. When we returned to Conza later that night, I presented each wrapped present. But I looked awkward, and so did they. My relatives are not people who place value on material goods, and the exchange only highlighted my difficulties in acknowledging their kindness. I felt very American, hoping that a little money could replace all those years of lost contact, and could partially excuse my family's absence from their lives.

The next morning we said good-bye to Concettina before returning to Avellino, our departure point for a few days of vacation in Rome. Throughout our stay in Conza, Concettina prepared our breakfast, cleaned up after us, ran about the kitchen in her black mourning dress talking in dialect, and, although two years younger than my own mother, briefly emerged as the grandmother tucked in my imagination. It was hard to say good-bye. Concettina hugged me, and with tears in her eyes said that she was an old woman and would probably not see us again. I pretended to disagree, but knew it was unlikely that we would return soon.

We piled into Franco's small car along with Gerardo and Franco's ten-year-old son Giovanni to head to Avellino. After a week of Franco's undivided attention, we found him preoccupied during our journey. It was a few days before I Morti, All Souls' Day, and an electrician was finally needed in Conza. Throughout the country, Italians pay tribute to the dead on this holiday by visiting their family cemeteries, and in the south villagers traditionally place a candle next to the graves of their loved ones. In a small gesture toward modernity, the families in Conza requested electric bulbs, resembling small Christmas tree lights, to shine continually on each tombstone. The town electrician had been called upon to make these lights.

When we arrived in Avellino, just in time for the Sunday *passeggiata*, the men from Conza were anxious on the benign streets. *Il piccolo paese è meglio*—a small town is better—Gerardo told me, who seemed comfortable only once during our final journey, at a gas-station stop we made along the way. Gerardo wandered off by himself as I was attempting to call our hotel in Rome. I spotted him far off in the distance, stooping on the black pavement. He walked back displaying a large grin and a bunch of arugula that had grown between the cracks, fresh-picked for his dinner salad. I thought about my dad pulling up dandelions many years before when he worked as a caddy; and observing Gerardo, I saw for myself how a countryman can find solace in the big town.

Avellino was a pretty city with a wide main street framed by trees planted on each side; their leaves moved like lovers in a forest, bidding and brushing the other. But I was disappointed as I watched dozens of short women with full faces take their *passeggiata* on this road, leisurely strolling beneath the emerald embrace of the trees; unlike what the man in the Piazza Navona had told me years before, I bore little resemblance to them. I looked more like the residents of Picerno, with their black-brown hair and solid angular noses.

Franco had to leave Avellino by 2:00 P.M. to work on the cemetery lights for I Morti. Back in Conza, Lucia and her eight-year-old son Michele were in the fields harvesting grapes. Concettina was waiting for mass to end at the church across the street from her home, hoping some parishioners would purchase the small purple clusters she had picked that morning.

In Rome we had a warm bed, terry robes, and good meals, but my husband and I admitted that, despite our complaints and discomfort, we were sorry to have left the warm embrace of my relatives, who had graciously welcomed us into their lives nearly a century after my grandfather abandoned this land. I told two of my Roman friends about the deprivation and lack of work in the south—how residents pounded laundry with a stone, and how burning wood was their sole source of heat. This activist couple who have aided African immigrants and studied black culture in the American South confessed embarrassment. The "southern problem" is largely ignored by the rest of Italy, tucked away after so many years of the region's inescapable poverty. Most Italians prefer not to ponder the south's intractable conditions until they are forced to, when an earthquake or mud slide becomes a major disaster because of shoddily built homes and the lack of preventive measures.

WHEN I SHED TEARS in the graveyard in Picerno, I was unaware of a history I shared with the Laurino women. My travel plan in southern Italy suited the story that I chose to tell: my profound emotional connection to my mother led me to her parents' town, where I retrieved a part of the Conte/Conti past. Cousin to cousin, Concetta and Connie, Natalia and Natalie, the two Marias, our names matched one another's and I placed meaning in the symmetry. Time also favored tracking down my mother's side since my father's first cousins are probably no longer alive. My father, whose own father was born in 1875, is six years older than my mother, and he is the second-youngest of seven children, all of whom have died.

But this partial history felt complete to me. My father's reserve and distance have made emotional encounters rare, while my mother and I have spent a lifetime engaged in the certainty that we are a part of the other, which we have wanted either to embrace or to escape. Discovering I was pregnant before the trip and pondering our family history afterward reinforced this feeling; it is the inheritance of our mothers, not our fathers, that women imagine with each kick and turn in our bellies. So I chose to forget that we inherit more than cultural remnants and quirks of personality.

On a morning that will forever drift back into my consciousness (the certainty of darkness forcing its power upon me and then bursting like a rain cloud), I walked into a hospital emergency room, thirty-four and a half weeks pregnant, with clumps of blood the size of half grapes oozing from my gums. A nurse attached a cuff to my left arm to monitor my blood pressure every fifteen minutes. One hundred fifty-eight, one hundred sixty-seven, one hundred eighty-eight over one hundred and ten, my arteries pulsed. A doctor entered the room and brusquely announced that an emergency C-section had to be performed.

I was told that I had a rare type of preeclampsia. The condition is a pregnancy-induced form of hypertension, and my uncommon syndrome was named, aptly, HELLP (the acronym stands for *h*emolysis, *e*levated *l*iver enzymes, and *l*ow *p*latelet count). The week before, I had been sitting in my doctor's office with normal blood pressure, normal fetal heartbeat, normal everything; now my baby and I had an uphill battle. My blood pressure soared; my kidneys and liver were shutting down, impeding my blood from clotting; my forearms turned black and blue as my veins spasmed and rejected IV needle after needle. We had about forty-eight hours, my doctor told me, before the medication for my blood pressure would cease to be effective. A perinatologist suggested putting off the operation until nighttime to stabilize my blood pressure and to try to induce labor, risky as it was to operate on someone whose blood barely clots. But the induction failed and by midnight I was being wheeled into the operating room, asked by a nurse if I wanted to see a priest.

"You had bad luck," an internist told me and my husband a week after the operation, the first time I was able to discuss the incident without crying or getting a nosebleed from my still-elevated blood pressure. I went to his office for a blood pressure check during a break from nursing my baby, born at three pounds fifteen ounces and lying in the hospital's neonatal intensive care unit. I agreed with the doctor, eager to interpret my illness as a random turn of bad events.

A few weeks later, I called a relative, who hadn't even heard that I was pregnant (my parents kept the news secret, afraid that Henry would get upset), to tell her about the birth.

"Didn't your dad tell you about Grandma Laurino?"

"No, what about her?"

My grandmother had suffered from preeclampsia, as had her daughter and her daughter's daughters. That afternoon I learned that I was fifth in a line of Laurino women who shared this disease. My grandmother and her daughter had each lost a baby to preeclampsia; my cousin had had a stillborn baby at eight months; her sister had gone into convulsions during labor, delivering a premature four-pound baby and causing the mother to nearly lose her life.

"You don't know how lucky you are," said my cousin, who also suffered from the disease.

My eighty-two-year-old dad did not remember his mother's childbearing illnesses; the rest were family secrets kept by my cousins, sad relics of the past dusted off and handed to me nearly fifty years later. There's little understanding of what triggers preeclampsia, the leading cause of fetal and maternal death, but since the lethal imbalance takes place within the placenta, removing the baby from the mother's body, no matter how early in gestation, is the only known cure.

What kind of inheritance is this that causes nature to thwart nature, and universally links me to the Laurino women of southern Italy? I will never know the terror and pain of my ancestresses who lay on prickly mattresses or hard wooden floors in those moments between the rhythmic wails of labor and the convulsions that electrified their bodies. I will never know how many of the Laurino women lying in that cemetery were victims of preeclampsia, having suffered seizures, stroke, and coma—the natural progression of this disease without medical care; this connection that I would discover in childbearing, quietly borne by generations before me, swaddled in family secrecy. What kind of luck do I have, inheritor and survivor?

Beginnings

ONCE MANY, MANY YEARS ago, my grandparents escaped the abysmal poverty of southern Italy when they boarded ships for America. They tried to leave behind the sadness of their land, but this lachrymose history could not be erased, it was part of them. They would bring the stories and traditions of this land, they would carry the effects of its deprivation and misery. I once refused to listen to these stories. I refused to enter the black-cloaked world of the peasants and discover my relationship to it. Now I can never fully enter or recover that world. But each time I denied its existence, embarrassed to stand out, monochrome in my neediness, I lost something irreplaceable, a texture of the soul.

"Recognize your root and your crown as of equal importance," wrote Robertson Davies in *The Rebel Angels*. He was describing his protagonist Maria, who had exchanged her swirling, spirit-filled, colorful half-Gypsy past for a staid, rational, laudably bland persona as a medieval scholar. A monk who becomes

Maria's spiritual guide admonishes her: "I think you are trying to suppress it because it is the opposite of what you are trying to be—the modern woman, the learned woman, the creature wholly of this age and this somewhat thin and sour civilization. . . . But you can't, you know. My advice to you, my dear, is to let your root feed your crown."

What a simple tale: I am part of a past.

Acknowledgments

TELLING STORIES THAT ARE a part of family history is a difficult task—by choosing what to include and in reshaping the story, the teller for the most part reveals his or her viewpoint. I want to thank the members of my extended family who generously took the time to provide details for some of the anecdotes in this book, and I hope that I rendered their accounts faithfully. My deepest gratitude to my parents and my brothers for giving me a sense of my culture, and myself; and for providing me with access to the tools to observe the blend of love and tradition, a sometimes combustible combination, that ultimately evolved into respect and acceptance in one Italian-American family. My brother Bob in particular continues to be a beacon to me and my family, and I thank him for his love and devotion.

I am indebted to the many people—scholars, psychologists, school administrators, politicians (especially former New York City Council member Sal Albanese), and fellow Italian-Americans and Italians (particularly Cristina Mattiello and Paolo Rondo Brovetto)—who shared ideas and viewpoints that are presented in the pages of this book.

Many friends have been family during the course of talking, thinking about, and writing this book: Matthew Belmont, Jennifer Brown (whose generosity and good humor have spanned three decades of friendship), and her husband Vincent Santoro. Lisa Bernhard, Jean Connolly, Renée Khatami, Susan Jacobson and David Moskovitz were always available and willing to lend a sympathetic ear. Over much broken bread and many raised glasses, Ruth Pastine and Gary Lang offered thoughts on works in progress. Sylvia and Earl Shorris provided needed hand-holding, tales from the published side, and invaluable ideas. Susan Klebanoff was a guardian angel. Michael's beloved "Sisi" enabled me to write in the mornings; Donna Brodie and the good folks at the Writers Room supplied the quiet to work. My dear pals and colleagues Annette Fuentes and LynNell Hancock knew how to revel in my enthusiasm and assuage my anxieties. Lucia Fiori and Robert Orsi generously read my manuscript, and I prize their insights and critiques, and their years of friendship.

My agent, Loretta Barrett, was a boundless source of enthusiasm and encouragement.

My editor, Alane Salierno Mason, believed in this project from its inception, understood the subject matter, and tenderly and painstakingly made this a better book.

My son, Michael, who came into being as this book began, is my primary source of wonder and beauty, and from him I learn more each day.

And finally, there are not enough ways to thank my husband Tony, my most trusted reader and adviser, who heard my thoughts about this subject during our first dinner together and attentively unfolded them in the continuing conversation of our marriage. His love, sensitivity, and intelligence not only helped me elevate an idea into a book but have made me a fuller person.